"All of us who were raised in the United States car_____ _____ from our White Supremacist culture, but those carried by BIPOC (Black, Indigenous, People of Color) are particularly onerous and are triggered on a daily basis. I know of no book that better describes this sad condition and presents a variety of practical ways for people to unburden than this one."

—**Richard Schwartz, PhD**, developer of the Internal Family
Systems Model, and adjunct faculty in the department of
psychiatry at Harvard Medical School

"Natalie helps us unpack and understand how systems of oppression contribute to our imposter syndrome and attachment wounds. The journal prompts and meditation guides lovingly bring us back to ourselves and connect us with our ancestors. A must-read for our souls' healing."

—**Alyssa Mancao, LCSW**, licensed clinical social worker,
writer, and owner of Alyssa Marie Wellness Inc. located in
Los Angeles, CA

"*The Pain We Carry* is the kind of book they should've assigned us in our multicultural counseling class... It is a rare, systems-centered book written by a therapist and thought leader needed for our times. The book offers a blend of stories (not focused on White identities), education, and practice—and that is sure to fill in the gaps that your grad school program left behind."

—**Oumou Sylla**, NYS-licensed therapist and wellness doula,
and founder of Joko Wellness LLC

"In *The Pain We Carry*, you will find Natalie's heart and spirit spilled out onto every page. Not only does she provide a practical framework and concrete exercises that expand hearts and deepen our individual healing journeys, but the compassion with which she guides us toward collective healing is unmatched in any other work. This is a true labor of love for our community and our humanity."

—**Leslie Priscilla**, latinx parenting founder, parent coach, facilitator, consejera, first-generation Xicana, and mother of three

"Every word in *The Pain We Carry* is intentional, powerful, and vulnerable. Natalie has beautifully crafted a book for racial trauma understanding and healing for survivors using knowledge grounded in anti-racism, parts work, and de-pathologizing language. This book is a wholesome contribution to the field of psychology and trauma recovery expertise."

—**Adriana Alejandre**, trauma therapist, founder of Latinx Therapy, and president of the Alejandre Foundation

"Stunning and soulful! This book is an essential tool to understand and heal intergenerational trauma. It offers simple-to-use skills to achieve and maintain optimal living in present-day toxic environments this trauma has produced. Our own healing and resilience become the most effective pathway for evolving ourselves, family, community, nation, and world. Written for and embracing BIPOC survivors, it is a gem for anyone wanting to understand, heal, and transform."

—**J. Eric Gentry, PhD, FAAETS**, forty-year veteran of working with survivors of trauma, developer of Forward-Facing Trauma Therapy, and director of five trauma-training/ certifying organizations

"Congratulations to Natalie for writing an outstanding book on such an important topic. This book sheds light on complex trauma in BIPOC, and offers useful tools in caring for yourself within external constraints."

—**Frank Anderson, MD,** author of *Transcending Trauma*

The Social Justice Handbook Series

As culture evolves, we need new tools to help us cope and interact with our social world in ways that feel authentic and empowered. That's why New Harbinger created the *Social Justice Handbook* series—a series that teaches readers how to use practical, psychology-based tools to challenge and transform dominant culture, both in their daily lives and in their communities.

Written by thought leaders in the fields of psychology, sociology, gender, and ethnic studies, the *Social Justice Handbook* series offers evidence-based strategies for coping with a broad range of social inequities that impact quality of life. As research has shown us, social oppression can lead to mental health issues such as depression, anxiety, trauma, lowered self-esteem, and self-harm. These handbooks provide accessible social analysis as well as thoughtful activities and exercises based on the latest psychological methods to help readers unlearn internalized negative messages, resist social inequities, transform their communities, and challenge dominant culture to be equitable for all.

The handbooks also serve as a hands-on resource for therapists who wish to integrate an understanding and acknowledgment of how multiple social issues impact their clients to provide relevant and supportive care.

For a complete list of books in
the *Social Justice Handbook* series,
visit newharbinger.com

The
Pain
We Carry

Healing from Complex PTSD
for People of Color

NATALIE Y. GUTIÉRREZ, LMFT

New Harbinger Publications, Inc.

Publisher's Note

NEW HARBINGER PUBLICATIONS is a registered trademark of New Harbinger Publications, Inc.

New Harbinger Publications is an employee-owned company.

Cover design by Sara Christian

Acquired by Georgia Kolias

Edited by Rona Bernstein

Library of Congress Cataloging-in-Publication Data

Names: Gutiérrez, Natalie Y., author.
Title: The pain we carry : healing from complex PTSD for people of color : reclaiming
    wholeness despite the burdens of systemic, intergenerational, and attachment trauma
    / Natalie Y. Gutiérrez, LMFT.
Other titles: Healing from complex PTSD for people of color
Description: Oakland, CA : New Harbinger Publications, [2022] | Series: The social
    justice handbook series | Includes bibliographical references.
Identifiers: LCCN 2022018818 | ISBN 9781684039319 (trade paperback)
Subjects: LCSH: Post-traumatic stress disorder--Popular works. | Post-traumatic stress
    disorder--Alternative treatment. | Stress (Psychology)--Popular works. | Minorities--
    Mental health. | BISAC: SELF-HELP / Post-Traumatic Stress Disorder (PTSD) |
    PSYCHOLOGY / Psychopathology / Post-Traumatic Stress Disorder (PTSD)
Classification: LCC RC552.P67 G88 2022 | DDC 616.85/210089--dc23/eng/20220705
LC record available at https://lccn.loc.gov/2022018818

Printed in the United States of America

26   25   24

10   9   8   7   6   5   4   3

To my children, your children, *our* children.

To my inner seven-year-old, thank you. Go play. I'll lead our way now.

To my rage, I hear you. You make sense. You are welcome here.

To our ancestors, who read this through your eyes,
we are because you were...

Contents

Foreword

We live in a world where humanity collectively continues to struggle with inexplicable loss, the burden of deep shame, and difficulty maintaining healthy forms of intimacy. Historical and intergenerational suffering have been shouldered by BIPOC for centuries. However, with the pandemic, and widespread public displays of racialized violence, what was once dismissed by "mainstream America" is now beckoning to be digested and addressed: it is time for global action. This begins with collective healing.

As someone who facilitates, teaches, and holds space for big emotions, my life's work is not just as a clinical psychologist, but also as a midwife for people who desire more from the therapeutic relationship: Work through those big feelings. Embody that rage. Make space for the deep grief. Create relationships with your ancestors. Figure out who you were prior to the touch of colonization. In founding Decolonizing Therapy, I discovered a part of myself that wanted so badly for the mental health systems to meet me, to hold grief for me, to show me what adults couldn't give me.

I recall one of our passionate car conversations where Nat said, "The mental health system is incomplete." My response: "It sure is." Who exactly do these systems serve? We were clear: they didn't serve people like us well. Natalie has dedicated much of her life to holding the parts in people that they are often too overwhelmed, overworked, and fearful to hold. She has articulated the effects of racial trauma on the well-being and souls of People of Color, our descendants, and our cultures in this book.

The Pain We Carry offers a lens into the deepest recesses of trauma: how it shows up and how it affects our relationships, well-being, and the way that safety appears to often evade our Brown and Black bodies. The book makes me smile and feel seen as a psychologist of color, as someone who teaches about Sacred Righteous Rage and the importance of honoring this sacred and vital emotion. This book offers a lens on humanizing emotions and working with them, rather than against them. From identifying our states of activation to understanding the intense effects of toxic stress on our bodies and psyches, this book brings us back into our bodies. It humanizes attachment wounding and offers teachings and exercises that allow for a connection to our emotions, humanity, and ancestry.

I trust that this book and these practices will bring all who read it relief from suffering and a head start toward the process of needing to peel in order to heal.

—Dr. Jennifer Mullan
"*The Rage Doctor*"
Founder, Decolonizing Therapy

Racism Has Stolen Our Emotional Safety

Dear Survivor. Let's start this conversation with a reminder: YOU are a resilient soul. If you've never been told this, I'm so glad you're here so I can tell you. I have so much gratitude for you, and your openness, as we begin this healing journey together. I want to say that I know some of you might be so tired of being resilient. That resilience has felt exhausting, that having to be strong has depleted many of your inner resources, and what you truly wish for is peace and safety.

Shit has been really rough, hasn't it? I'm thinking of your heart right now. As I write this book, I deeply wish things were better for you—and all our communities. Things haven't felt "good" for a while. Part of me really wishes I knew all the right words to say to make all your pain go away. Heck, I wish I even knew those words for myself. I'm writing this book during a time that's been quite challenging for all of us, and by the time it's published, I don't know what more will have happened. I write this book with the lens of today, holding hope in my heart for tomorrow. I offer this book to you not knowing exactly what's going on in your life right now, but wanting to be a pillar of strength for you.

I also want to say that you might feel uncomfortable as you're reading when I say hard things about police brutality or White supremacy, especially if you're a member of law enforcement, White, or other dominant groups (or have close proximity to them). Or perhaps a perspective of mine here differs from yours. And that's okay. Your discomfort and ambivalence are welcome here. Journey with them as you begin to take the risk of opening your heart more to your experience. Your discomfort isn't danger-ous, and it has the ability to break you open to loving and seeing differ-ently. Our discomfort can help make us aware of our biases and enable us to see our own vulnerability and that of others. Just know that all that's written here comes from a place of love and openheartedness for you.

So much harm continues to be inflicted on Black and Brown commu-nities. State-sanctioned violence is an oppressive system, perpetuating racism on Black, Indigenous, and People of Color. We are people living in Black and Brown skin feeling unsafe to be ourselves. Who and how we are is on my mind: Black and Brown queer; neurodivergent with various abili-ties wondering if you'll ever belong; cisgender, nonbinary, trans; all who feel lonely and disconnected from themselves; those among us with racial-ized identities and lineages harmed for centuries by racism, genocide, war, and colonization.

I want to take a moment to pause and honor the collective grief for all Indigenous children found buried in unmarked graves near several Canadian residential schools. This is the very devastating impact of geno-cide, colonization, forced assimilation, and White body supremacy on Indigenous peoples of Turtle Island. This is part of the painful legacies carried by Native Americans.

We continue feeling the brunt of harm from White body supremacy on our mind, body, and spirit. *All* Black folks, Indigenous folks, and People of Color (including mixed-race folks) are in my thoughts while I write. We're the global majority.

I'll be just as honest with you as I ask you to be with yourself. I've had a really hard time writing. I've been in my head a lot, which happens to be one of my survival tools. My sense of overwhelm in a world that's hurting all around me for as long as I can remember has kept me avoidant, protect-ing myself. I get stuck in my head, avoiding all the feelings in my heart—all to feel safer, even for one teeny moment. You've picked up this book, so you know what I mean about having survival tools when things are just too hard.

It's a privilege to go through life not having the way you express your-self or live your life be policed. It's a privilege to feel comfortable writing and speaking in your natural voice because the world hasn't tried to silence you. Internalized racism and classism have taught me to hate the way I speak. I struggled to write this book because I have lived afraid of what people might think of me and I was taught to shrink and silence my voice. Fear says I must prove everything I say to the White people who read this book, or they will judge me and maybe even try to dismiss my words. This happens often: Communities of Color are asked for burden of proof that racism still exists.

Can you relate to the fear and added burden around having enough "proof" structural racism is real and terribly impacts Black and Brown communities? There aren't enough books that can be written to fully speak to all the ways this is true. And because of that, like me, you're left defending your story and what you know to be true without all the "evidence."

How do you prove what you *know* to be true from lived experience? Literature can't back you up because there are fewer researchers and authors of the global majority. And how do you grow to accept and love your voice when the sound of your voice has been called ghetto, uneducated, and angry? At times I've found myself code-switching in my own writing, pandering to the White people who would read this to "prove" myself, when this very book is meant to be for *you*.

That is the insidiousness of White body supremacy. Code-switching (i.e., modifying your speech, accent, or vocabulary in the presence of White people) can sometimes be revered as folks' ability to assimilate, or fit in, among various groups (especially dominant groups). But code-switching can be stressful and results in loss of identity or self-rejection. I can tell you I've grown tired of being that palatable Latina they've wanted me to be. When you're having to be a chameleon that changes colors to match your environment for survival and in order to be accepted and loved…imagine what that does. Your heart breaks receiving explicit messages from groups in power—that the only way you will be truly loved and accepted is through assimilation. That shit cuts deep. So deep, it becomes trauma.

So let's talk about trauma for a moment. Trauma is the imprint of chronic, toxic stress in our minds and bodies. It's the powerlessness we feel when we cannot overcome something, or someone, causing us immense pain. Trauma robs us of our self-love and completely changes our sense of safety in the world. Trauma can be a single-incident experience or a series of painful incidents over time. It can start from before you were born, or at any stage in your life.

When your pain isn't met with love and support, your traumatic experience can lead to posttraumatic stress disorder (PTSD) or complex posttraumatic stress disorder (CPTSD). And, when it comes to experiences of racism and oppression, even when you receive love and support you can still develop PTSD or CPTSD, because feeling othered every day can rob you of your sense of safety in the world. As a Black, Indigenous, and Person of Color, you might find yourself struggling with accumulated trauma or prolonged exposure to traumatic experiences, including facing racial trauma, microaggressions, and marginalization regularly. Here are some ways you might experience this struggle:

- You might waver between depression and anxiety.

- You might experience despair, maybe even sometimes wanting to die.

- Your heart might race when you're stopped by police.

- You might experience intrusive thoughts and memories of times when you were discriminated against, called racial slurs or other oppressive slurs, or abused in any way.

- You might have mastered the survival technique of numbing out, or dissociating, to avoid feeling your feelings.

- You might feel like an imposter no matter how accomplished you are, and feel a constant sense of otherness.

This is CPTSD. You might already know this on a soul level. Let this serve as more confirmation and validation of what your heart already knows and might've just not had the words to describe. Sometimes the diagnosis CPTSD doesn't even fully encapsulate all the trauma Black and Indigenous peoples experience in the inside and outside world when there's still a cultural genocide happening. This book also welcomes you to allow yourself to define your trauma, and others to define theirs.

I don't know your exact trauma and I won't pretend that I do—but I know mine. I predict there's confluence in our pain. I want to tell you that you're not "crazy," and the whole reason I'm writing this book is because many Black folks, Indigenous folks, and Folks of Color are experiencing symptoms of CPTSD disguised as anxiety and depression (often even being misdiagnosed and misunderstood). I really want to validate that the pain you're feeling is very real and help you understand it.

First thing's first, though. I want to share that I have privilege, more than some people in my community because of colorism. I don't always feel the privilege when my intersectional identities meet an oppressive world and I'm confronted with racism, sexism, classism, and ableism. But I know I benefit from my light skin because even within our Black and Brown communities, we have different experiences based on the advantage given to lighter skin.

I also need to say that even this book isn't enough to speak to all of the pain you carry. It isn't lost on me that not all people of the global majority have the same experience culturally around the world. Just like Latine experiences aren't monolithic, the same is true for *all* racialized identities. Our experiences aren't universal. Especially for those of us reading this book who have lighter skin along with other intersecting identities (term coined by Kimberlé Crenshaw) that are also marginalized. Us light-skinned People of Color will never know what it's like to live in a Black body, and will never know all of the real dangers Black people face living in the US (and around the world). We will know some, but we won't know all. That's just the reality of racism and colorism, which create ruptures and painful dynamics between family when we're treated differently because of the hues of our skin.

On a similar note, we also share a lot, including the impacts of different historical trauma. Because we all have different experiences as the global majority, we will need more than just my book to tell the story of the pain carried by *all* People of Color. I put so much pressure on myself to have this book encapsulate all the pain that we carry until I realized that expectation was my own internalized White supremacy culture; I was expecting perfection and was never satisfied. But now I know in my soul that this book is meant to witness the pain we carry and to encourage us to continue writing this shared story for our communities. I surely cannot be the spokesperson for all. As we think about all the voices and stories we want represented in books, I hope you'll consider helping write them. This world needs your words too. I hope you will be inspired to write books that center the healing of your culture and speak to all the burdens you carry from Western and non-Western culture.

Much of the Latine identity today comes from past trauma. History reminds us of the colonization of the land belonging to Indigenous peoples in North, Central, and South America and the Caribbean, along with the Atlantic Slave Trade that eventually culminated in much of the Latine identity. My ancestors are a mix of Spaniard, African, and Taíno in Boríken. I come from a family of *curanderas* (spiritual healers) inspired by the African Yoruba tradition. Most have abandoned the practice due to its misassociation with evil.

For so long, I've had a thirst for connection to spiritual healing. You probably know this feeling too, robbed and disconnected from the healing practices of ancestors. They were said to be devil's work by White missionaries or settlers or slave traders. Many of our empowering and peaceful ancestral practices have been colonized and demonized. We have internalized messages that reject the very healing work curated by elders and ancestors. It's a privilege to even know your ancestors, as folks with lineages of genocide and enslavement have been disconnected from knowledge of their ancestry. That alone carries deep pain and grief. If this is your truth, even with the loss of your family's history, your ancestors live within you and aren't lost. *It's possible* to begin creating an ancestral practice, even from scratch—feeling for what intuitively comes up for you and trusting yourself as a guide.

I chose to do trauma work and trauma work also chose me. For over a decade, I've held many painful stories of Black and Brown bodies in my therapy office. The more years that passed, the clearer it became that suffering is tied to racialized trauma and systemic issues beyond my patients' control. Many would numb out the grief, rage, anxiety, and hurt they experienced daily from microaggressions, sexism, homophobia, transphobia, and ableism—depending on their intersectional identities. So much of how we define ourselves was learned from racist institutions. The mental health field wasn't doing enough to understand this, and was actually quicker to pathologize patients like mine—for example, referring to deep fears as paranoid or delusional. But here's what I was noticing:

Of course you feel afraid and distrustful when you live in a Black body and are approached by police. Your visceral bodily reactions happen because history shows implicit bias in a police state that has led to present-day lynching of Black bodies.

Of course you struggle with internalized racism and find it hard to feel self-acceptance. You've been taught to criticize who you are, how you look, how much space you take up, ways you show up. Even the way you speak is policed. You survive by remaining very aware of how you might be perceived by folks of dominant groups, because being othered or seen as dangerous due to racism and implicit bias is life-threatening when you're existing in a Black or Brown body.

Of course you feel anger, anxiety, and grief after so many generations experiencing racial trauma in your family. You have legacy wounds from genocide, enslavement, war, and colonization.

Your pain makes sense. You make sense.

I want to take a moment to appreciate the work of Dr. Joy Degruy. In her book *Post Traumatic Slave Syndrome*, she writes a deep history of how the era of enslavement has gravely impacted Black bodies, and how centuries of enslavement continue to impact Black folks today. I also want to honor the work of Resmaa Menakem, whose book *My Grandmother's Hands* has also illuminated the somatic impact of racialized trauma. They've helped inspire my own learning, growth, and humility. If these works are unfamiliar to you, please seek them on your healing journey.

For quite some time, my rage was how I protected myself from the world and how I learned to communicate my needs through intimidation and aggression. Seeing violence in my home taught me to resolve conflict through fighting and to get my needs met through yelling or hitting. I also learned to anticipate violence, gauging the moods of my parents and others so that I could know how to avoid confrontation—whether through shrinking myself and playing small, people pleasing, or fighting back—all to emotionally and physically survive. And then I grew to become a teenager who was raging and angry with the world, feeling a fiery anger inside that sometimes turned to outward expressions of explosive anger. All while the world told me to exile my rightful rage. I had so many reasons to be rageful. I now know my rage was trying to call out for help. It needed a witness. My rage wanted the hurt to stop, from the world and in my home.

You might know what growing up seeing violence in the home as a child feels like, with your hurt and anger unwitnessed, shamed, and invalidated. Your anger may have kept people away as a form of protection and anticipatory self-defense. Your anger may feel responsible and burdened to keep you safe in a world that has hurt you and your ancestors. Today I make a conscious effort to continue getting to know my rage so that it doesn't take me over and leak out on to the people I love. I continue to try and take the risk of being vulnerable with others.

Vulnerability hasn't come easy for me, and I'm sure you can relate to that. When you're trying to take a risk and be vulnerable, you might find yourself feeling tense and anticipating that bad things will happen. When you've lived through childhood trauma and betrayal, your brain reminds you that vulnerability can lead to more pain, so we tend to create all kinds of armor against it.

Many of us often perceive threat in our environments, exacerbated by living in a structurally racist and violent society that repeatedly oppresses non-White groups. We tend to struggle trusting others, including people in our own communities, and even ourselves. We might even unconsciously become our own oppressors and continue mistreating ourselves and others, including our friends, partners, and children.

We can find ourselves perpetuating the very systems of oppression and abuse in our own homes, within our own minds and bodies, families, and communities, taught to us by White supremacy. This might look like screaming at our loved ones and hitting or shaming our children. This might look like invalidating and shaming the vulnerability in others. We can no longer hide behind our wounds if we are to foster healing within and in our communities. We cannot dismiss or minimize violence in the home or toward our communities as "normal" or believe that we are fine despite being physically hurt by our caregivers or anybody. I assure you we are *not* fine.

We've struggled in relationships, with setting boundaries, and with our own self-worth. Somewhere within us exists rage, insecurity, and resentment—deeply rooted. I can admit to you that growing up in a household where I was often hit produced the rage I still carry today. It has been flamed by the many other times I experienced traumatic stress and betrayal as a child by adults I trusted. Yet I chose to do my healing work to end the pattern for future generations. Every day I choose to still take this healing journey; the ancestors aren't done with me yet.

The legacy burdens of abuse passed down in your family can stop with you. It can all begin to shift in this lifetime, at least the part within your control. There may be a part of you that wonders, *How can I ever let down my guard in a country that doesn't want me, or that continuously makes me feel physically and emotionally unsafe?* Quite frankly, I'm not sure that the answer is to entirely let down your guard or remove your armor. Rather, the answer seems to include intentionally creating moments of self-reflection, connecting to yourself and with others you trust or want to learn to trust. It means offering yourself the same compassion that you're so good at giving to others and not as comfortable giving to yourself. You can practice tending to yourself with four empowered steps to heal in body, mind, spirit, and intention.

The Cultural Empowerment Approach to Healing

I developed this approach through my own personal work and the inspiration I've received from the communities I've served over the years. This approach to healing from complex, racism-driven trauma and CPTSD, which you will learn in this book, will not end racism or oppression—I wish it were that powerful. What it *will* do is provide you with a powerful and effective tool kit to find personal healing from trauma, stress, grief, and the painful weight of existing in an oppressive society, and a renewed sense of strength and resilience to go on living. It's designed to empower you to navigate this world and claim your healing through self- and community care.

The goal is for you to be able to show up in your life as your truest Self (the you without all the pain you carry) and live your life's purpose as you work to change the very inequitable system that has disrupted your life and invalidated your pain and struggle. In order to truly create societal change, we need to make sure we no longer internalize the messages of an oppressive society and become our own oppressor. We must make sure we're not becoming our own enemy by mistreating ourselves because we've internalized racism (and other isms, like sexism, classism, ableism, ageism, heterosexism, transphobia, and fatphobia).

I created the cultural empowerment approach to healing to help those who've been marginalized and traumatized due to their race and culture (and other discriminatory factors) to *reclaim their wellness holistically* and unapologetically. Cultural legacy burdens, or the oppressive beliefs and energy inherited from the larger culture, are painful to internalize. Finding the motivation to heal from them can be difficult when you're consistently betrayed by the societal institutions and people around you, which is why the basis of this approach focuses on what you *can* trust and control: your physical body, your thoughts, and your actions. This approach seeks to empower you, to instill hope and genuine expectancy for a resilient future, and to whisper faith back into your spirit.

The holistic offering of the cultural empowerment approach to healing includes:

- Customized practices designed to overcome the cultural legacy burdens you carry, the oppression and hardships you journey through daily, and your own internalized narrative influenced by racism.

- Direction for acknowledging your rightful rage—a rage that's sacred, passed down from your ancestors along with the cumulative loss and grief caused by widespread oppression against Black folks, Indigenous folks, and other Folks of Color for centuries.

- Evidence-based practices that, while not always widely known in mainstream psychotherapy and the society at large today, have been shown to work in ways that truly heal the complexities of the traumas we face.

This book has a four-part structure. In each part you will find a story and reflection, some education and practices, and an empowerment step. Each empowerment step is designed to heal you from the inside out and—with dedicated application and practice—help you build and reconnect to your resilience. Here are the four empowerment steps laid out in this approach:

Use Your Body to Regulate Your Own Well-Being: The traumatic stress of racism compounded by everyday perceived threats keeps your body in its instinctual survival mode—fight-or-flight—for far longer than is necessary and healthy, eventually wreaking havoc on your nervous system. Self-regulation *interrupts* this fight-or-flight response, restoring your body to comfort and your brain to optimal cognitive functioning. This step is all about becoming fluent in the "language" of your body, meaning the sensations you feel in your body before you release pent-up tension and return yourself to stability and centeredness—especially in those moments when the world feels scary, stressful, and dangerous.

Mend Shame and Shaming Beliefs with Self-Compassion: Once you can properly regulate your body, you regain the ability to address any hurtful ways of thinking with grace and self-compassion. You'll learn to ground yourself in times of fear, replace your negative beliefs with positive ones, and honor the inner child and survivor within you by thanking them for having brought you through your trauma. This step focuses on fostering the belief that you *do* possess the inner strength necessary to heal yourself, a strength that's already been proven by your survival and the survival of your ancestors. It integrates techniques from an internal family systems therapeutic modality to help you better understand your inner world and all parts of you that exist internally that feel vulnerable or protective and carry burdens.

Access the Energy of Your Ancestors' Wisdom: Reconnecting with your ancestral spirit is the third step in this revolutionary approach to reclaiming and healing from trauma. The reality is that many of us in the global majority have been estranged from the communities and heritages that are our birthright in ways large and small. Maybe they were mocked and ridiculed by people we knew, and so we separated ourselves from them. Maybe we sensed that in order to survive or live a life with some stability and prosperity in a racist nation, we needed to conform to the White, Christian, middle-class norm—and distance ourselves from anything out of that norm, including the recognition of our ancestors, their hardships, and how they survived and thrived through it all.

When this disconnect occurs, it leaves you without those supports that would otherwise sustain you: the knowledge that those like you faced the same things you did and endured; supportive presences from the past you can turn to when life is hard and you feel yourself being dehumanized; and models for a life that's authentically yours. This step of the approach entails "returning home to yourself" by replacing unhealthy routines with beneficial ones, and rekindling your relationship with your ancestors through their wisdom and healing practices. These sources of gentle support and ritual will provide comfort and a never-ending supply of resilience to weather the repeated challenges you'll continue to face in an oppressive world.

Live Intentionally to Change an Unjust System: This fourth and final step provides you with a set of tools inspired by Forward-Facing® trauma therapy, a form of therapy that deals with trauma head-on in order to reclaim personal integrity, self-worth, and joy. This step will enable you to identify the person you *want* to be while navigating challenges. Here you will define your life mission, constructing a detailed framework that will help guide your actions based on what *you* want to do and be, as you challenge systems of oppression by living authentically and aligned to your values, not by what a racist society or the trauma you've endured has taught you to do and be. This intentionality of behavior ensures you're living in your most authentic Self, maintaining your integrity, and defining yourself based on *your* perceptions—not replaying the internalized messages of systemic racism. This step encourages you to reclaim your joy as a form of resistance. It's important for your healing that you live aligned with your values, principles, passions, and personal mission, instead of allowing this society's oppressive systems to rob you of your life's purpose.

Preparation for Healing

Before we go further, I'll lay some groundwork so you can get the most out of this book. The practices you'll find throughout the text encourage self-reflection and real-world application. Do them at whatever pace feels right for you. Not every practice will resonate with you, and that's okay. Healing isn't a one-size-fits-all process, so choose what feels best for you and go with that. Trust your process and use your intuition as your guide.

For all the meditation and a few other practices, you can download an audio recording from the website for this book, http://www.newharbinger .com/49319. (See the very back of this book for more details.)

When you sit down to practice, find a quiet space where you can focus, offering patience and loving-kindness to yourself as you (un)learn and grow. If you're able, have a notebook and writing utensil nearby, or any device and application you feel comfortable dictating your notes on. These will be valuable tools for your processing and internal work and, in time, a record of your growth and progress as you heal.

It's important to me that everyone can access this healing work, so feel free to tweak the practices to suit your style and needs. There are many ways you can do the practices in this book. You can choose to do them as you're reading, or focus on one of the steps weekly or monthly if it feels like too much. You can also choose to practice as part of a group in the community, with a book club, or separately with friends. One of my goals with this book is to get you to look inward and begin listening to what you need and what works best for you. This can be a great start as you continue reconnecting with yourself.

Lastly, delving into your prior trauma(s) requires care and lots of self-check-ins. If any of the following apply to you, *please* reach out to professionals and/or get to a safe place before beginning my four-step approach to healing:

- You're a survivor of multiple severe traumatic experiences.

- You're having thoughts of suicide or self-harm.

- You're not safe, or do not feel physically safe.

- You don't have the basic necessities for safe and healthy living.

I invite you to refer to the list at the back of the book for resources that can aid you in receiving proper care and establishing safe surroundings, as this is of the utmost importance as you get started.

My wish for you is to reclaim your self-love, your self-compassion, your self-care, your self-acceptance, your power, your nervous system, your body, your ancestral wisdom and healing, your community's care, and your sense of belonging within it. To heal ourselves is to heal the generations that have come before us and to create a ripple effect for the ones that will come after. Our collective healing is imperative in this lifetime. Releasing the ancestral trauma and cultural legacy burdens carried in our minds, bodies, and spirits isn't just some radical and idealistic idea—it's surely our *only* route to liberation and wholeness. So let's travel this road together, through this book.

PART I

Trauma Is Written into Our Black and Brown Bodies

If there's one universal truth that we in the United States, and around the world, can agree upon today, it's this: *racism is real, and it's traumatizing.* Regardless of the claims of those who say that "slavery is over; just let it go!" or the high school history books that exclude details of the grave injustices and genocide committed against Indigenous people as our nation was formed, racism is undeniably part of our world history and it is present in all aspects of the US today.

Over the centuries and even longer, Black, Indigenous, and People of Color have been oppressed and marginalized, forced to conform and "fit the White mold" even when beloved facets of their cultures were appropriated for White consumption. Immigrants and refugees have been stereotyped or told they "have good English for a foreigner"; Black and Brown folks have found their appearances and their behavior scrutinized and policed; Asian Americans have been the recipients of pointed racist remarks since news of the COVID-19 pandemic broke, just as practicing Muslims who wear headscarves and hijab are often the targets of racial profiling and verbal abuse in public spaces after being stereotyped as terrorists following September 11th.

How many times have you been hurt by racism and its toxic effects in your own day-to-day life? As a Latina myself, I've internalized so much about who I am, who I should be, how I should look and speak, and what's acceptable or not from the things I've seen and heard growing up in a racist world that also looks down on people financially struggling. Simply put, *it was never okay to just be me*—and sometimes it wasn't even safe. As a Black, Indigenous, and Person of Color yourself, you might find that you're living in perpetual states of fear, grief, and rage because of the profoundly painful pasts your communities and ancestors have experienced. And this trauma—or more appropriately, this *traumatic grief* characterized by the loss of safety, basic freedoms and dignities, equal opportunities, and even actual *lives* in this society—is passed down through the generations. How can it not be? I want you to ask yourself:

- How does it feel in my body and how does it hurt me when I see the suffering of people who look like me?

- How does being in a Black or Brown body within racist systems impact my sense of safety in the world?

- How does it impact expectations of myself?

- How does it impact how I show up for myself and what I tell myself about me?

As you're carrying these wounds of loss and grief, your physical and mental energy may feel depleted from spending so many hours of each day trying to prove you're worthy of basic human rights in a world that thinks and says otherwise. And your spirit is probably burdened by constantly being othered. And to top it all off, all the ancestral practices that historically brought comfort and stability were put aside or forgotten altogether with seemingly no prospects for the relief of your suffering because somewhere along the line your elders or ancestors were forced to surrender them.

That racism you've experienced living in this oppressive system has caused traumatic stress. There are clear forms of oppression that you can *certainly* call out as oppression—like our nation's blatant police brutality and unlawful uses of force against Black and Brown people. And there are also many other ways oppression shows itself in the form of discrimination, such as in

- the lack of Black and Brown representation in TV shows and movies (and who gets to act in them);

- the predominantly White, cisgender dolls and action figures sold on department store shelves;

- magazines and books (and who gets their work published or not);

- corporate structures, wages, and promotional opportunities;

- restricted access to water, healthy food, medical care, and other things we all need to live;

- restricted access to financial resources to afford housing and higher education;

- media coverage that is more compassionate to the suffering of White bodies over Black and Brown bodies; and

- the disparity and favorability of White refugees over Black and Brown refugees around the world.

We're taught from very early ages, through lack of representation, restricted access, and being told we're not welcomed, to not take up space. Our needs, feelings, and presence don't matter. And when we feel like we don't matter, we feel vulnerable and write ourselves off in one way or another. We might dismiss our own needs and internalize the cultural burden placed on us that says we just don't matter. And that message continues to have ripple effects on the generations that come after us, becoming legacy burdens.

Yet even as discrimination, oppression, and violence have prevailed in this country and around the world, it's *absolutely possible* to reclaim yourself in a system rigged against you. It's possible to learn to understand your own body, comfort yourself, and regulate the stress you so often feel. It's possible to feel compassion for yourself and others for the ways you've suffered, and to feel genuine self-love. It's possible to see the value you hold as someone of the global majority and to commit to living by those values, as best you can, even in this racist world. And it's possible to honor your family and your ancestors by breaking the intergenerational cycle of trauma and reconnecting with the rituals of your ancestry.

You *can* reclaim what the trauma of racism has taken from you: calm and ease in your own body, clarity and intention in your life, and the resources of your ancestors that are yours to inherit. In order to do this, I think we need to really understand cultural legacy burdens and how they are passed down and show up without us even knowing. In chapter 1, I'll introduce you to Terrence, and you'll see how cultural legacy burdens are part of his daily experience. Then, in chapter 2, we'll look at the physical and psychological impact of cultural legacy burdens. And in chapter 3, we'll cover the first empowerment step, where I'll invite you to reflect on any cultural legacy burdens you're holding so you can begin to know them better and get a sense of how they show up for you personally.

CHAPTER 1

Terrence's Story (he/him)

Terrence is a thirty-two-year-old, cisgender Black man living in Washington, DC, in late May of 2020. He deals with the reminders of systemic racism and oppression all day, every day, from the moment he leaves his apartment to when he returns. Here's how.

Terrence often receives dirty looks in the coffee shop nearby his workplace, and the cashiers regularly mispronounce his name, even though he has corrected them many times. He's sometimes followed by a squad car in the evening as he gets off the subway to go home, which gets his heart pounding with fear that he'll be stopped and accused of walking while Black. He has heard people mutter racial slurs at him in stores. In graduate school, Terrence was often told White privilege wasn't real, even though he was receiving less grant money than his White peers every year.

Terrence regularly struggled with fear and anxiety and held tension in his body as a result of the pain he was running from. Terrence anticipated microaggressions daily. His anxiety caused him bouts of insomnia, a racing pulse, and migraines, and he always felt on edge—toggling between wanting to fight back or run away at any moment. But where would he go to feel safe in the world? Racism lives everywhere.

Terrence financially supported his mom. Terrence's father had been physically abusive to his mother and verbally abusive to him when he was young, criticizing Terrence's complexion. Terrence blames himself for not having protected his mother from his father's bouts of rage and abuse when he was a child, and deals with depression and shame from his dad that made him hate himself. He also internalized society's racist messages about

Black men; he feels like he has to work harder than others just to get to where they are and has learned he shouldn't rest.

The belief that resting was laziness was passed down throughout his family for generations. Rest was uncomfortable. Grind culture was heavily glorified in his family because of the belief that they were behind and needed to do the most to be seen as valuable. He learned self-worth through measuring his accomplishments, not by seeing his own inherent value.

To cope with all of his stress, he overexercised, overworked, and tried to distract himself from the deep-rooted pain he didn't allow himself to feel. It was safer to check out and be numb than it was to confront the world when his life was constantly being interrupted by racism. This is complex trauma.

Maybe just pause here for a breath, stretch, or do anything you need to do to care for yourself after taking in Terrence's story. Just notice what that was like to read. And come back when you're ready.

Shared Experience: Cultural Legacy Burdens and Oppression

The microaggressions Terrence was forced to confront from the moment he stepped out his front door to the moment he returned home aren't new, and aren't an isolated case of oppression—this is the reality for most Black people in the US, and for other Folks of Color as well (though many of us light-skin People of Color don't share these exact same experiences). And it's likely a reality for you. Do you recognize aspects of Terrence's struggle in your own life? Maybe you've endured the same indignities: suspicious glares from a stranger, fear of speaking up/having a voice, or the soul-piercing fear that local law enforcement will get involved in your life with just one misplaced step or phone call.

These experiences of chronic, prolonged exposure to racism and painful environments are *toxic stress* (a term originally coined by the National Scientific Council on the Developing Child to describe developmental trauma, broadened by Dr. Nadine Burke Harris to include ongoing exposure to adversity). Toxic stress can lead to complex posttraumatic stress disorder (CPTSD). If you found your body feeling tense as you read Terrence's story, this may very well be a clear sign of a trauma response within you.

Does your reaction make sense to you? CPTSD is a brain-and-body survival response that arises from the slew of situations you and folks in your community confront daily: racism, intergenerational trauma, homophobia, transphobia, sexism, ableism, sexual abuse, emotional abuse, and other violent and abusive experiences that continue to accumulate over periods of time and rob you of your sense of safety and stability in the world. This accumulation of ongoing traumatic experiences leads to CPTSD.

I'm not really a fan of the word "disorder," as this has some pathologizing tones—so I want you to know that you're not broken. Dr. Bruce Perry uses the phrase "post-traumatic injury,"[1] and I really appreciate the understanding that it isn't that you're flawed because of what happened, it's that you're hurt. Your reaction to racial trauma and oppression are valid for what is being done *to* you and what has been done *to* your people. The historical trauma of your ancestors that has been felt through colonization and land theft, genocide, enslavement, scientific racism, enduring war, and famine has left deep traumatic grief, rage, and shame. And for many generations the legacy burdens of this historical trauma have been passed down, compounded by the personal burdens you directly experience today living in a Black or Brown body.

Reflection

Now pause and take a deep breath, centering your attention on your own experience. When you're ready, ask yourself these two questions and take note of your responses, perhaps in your journal:

- What have I had to sacrifice (give up, change, or bury) within and outside myself just to exist safely in a racist world?

- When I experience a microaggression, what do I notice happening in my body?

Before moving on, let's take a brief moment to just check in with what's going on for you right now. What do you notice coming up around what you've taken into your heart so far? If it feels right, just take a deep breath and place your hand over your heart (wherever in your body you experience it) and tell yourself the words you most need to hear right now (maybe they're the words you wish someone had said to you). Things like "You matter" or " I love you" or "You are enough" or "It's okay to take up space" or "I get you." Give these words to yourself.

In the next chapter, you may feel your experience clarified as I shine some light on cultural legacy burdens. Seeing them is becoming aware of them, helping you better understand their impact on your self-esteem and choices.

CHAPTER 2

The Impact of Cultural Legacy Burdens on Our Bodies and Minds

You might have dealt with some (or many) traumatic experiences in your life. And due to these painful and perhaps prolonged occurrences, you have naturally developed negative beliefs about yourself and the world. These beliefs, and the energy accompanying them, are *burdens* that you internalize and carry within, both consciously and unconsciously, that dictate how connected, protected, and safe you feel—or don't feel. You can inherit these burdens from

- the larger culture (i.e., *cultural legacy burdens*)—these are sets of messages and beliefs you've absorbed from systemic racism and oppression;

- your family (i.e., *family legacy burdens*)—these narratives inform your family patterns and can breed family illness and mental health issues; and

- painful experiences that happened directly to you (i.e., *personal burdens*)—these include microaggressions, racial trauma, sexual abuse, neglect, assault, or any traumatic event you experienced.

Here we will focus primarily on cultural legacy burdens. We hold pain from the past and also interface with a society that continues to worsen these burdens. Let's talk more about this…

As a Black, Indigenous, and Person of Color struggling with CPTSD in the form of racial and historical trauma, you carry cultural legacy burdens that have shaped your thinking, your sense of self, and probably your worldview. And while burdens can also be personal—such as physical trauma in childhood that leads someone to subconsciously seek out abusive partners in adulthood—the burdens I'm talking about are large scale, permeating throughout this nation's society to directly disadvantage and hurt you and other marginalized groups. These cultural legacy burdens aren't yours. They belong to a system that has hurt your family and continues burdening you. The four most known—named by Richard Schwartz, developer of internal family systems therapy—are racism, patriarchy, materialism, and individualism (see figure 1).[2]

Still, please be aware of all the other isms causing injury to your heart: ableism, classism, ageism, sexism, transphobia, homophobia, fatphobia, xenophobia or discrimination based on immigration status, and many others. Each of these cultural legacy burdens can be easily visible or insidious, and all impact you in various damaging ways. Simply put, they comprise the hurtful stories carried in your body and mind from when other people and/or your environment has hurt you.

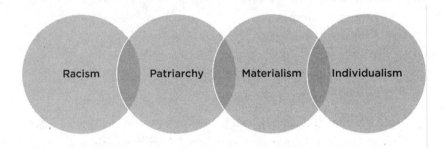

Figure 1: Four cultural legacy burdens.

Racism: Racism is at the core of all trauma and complex posttraumatic stress that you can experience as a Black, Indigenous, and Person of Color—even as you hold other marginalized identities. It's the structural foundation on which this country was built, used as a driving force to dehumanize and commit heinous crimes centuries ago (and today) against

Indigenous and Black bodies. It's the system that was designed to exercise power over Black and Brown bodies.

We are all born into this system, and the burden of racism affects us all in different ways. If you're living in a Black body, you probably have also experienced anti-Blackness from other People of Color. Colorism is definitely a painful personal burden fueled by the cultural burden of racism that's perpetuated within the Latine community, and other Communities of Color, where lighter skin has more advantage. The more you're able to pass as White, the more you can assimilate and be accepted by White culture.

There are three types of racism that reflect the different layers at which racist ideas and practices permeate society: systemic, institutional, and interpersonal (all creating the internalized racism within you). We'll delve deeper into the ways racist messaging on a societal level makes its way down into our soul in toxic environments, and how to hold on to yourself, in chapters 11 and 12.

Patriarchy: Patriarchy is the belief that cisgender men—men whose gender identity aligns with their sex at birth—are superior. All cisgender, or "cis," men benefit from this system to some degree, though patriarchal standards lean most favorably toward White cis men, since being a White man means you also receive the status that society assigns to being White.

Patriarchy at its most extreme supports rigid gender roles, hypermasculinity, homophobia, transphobia, and intimate partner violence. Patriarchy forges misogyny and transmisogyny (prejudice against transgender women). The way patriarchy influences the Latine community is through machismo—with cis men having more power, privilege, and entitlement (while also being forced to reject their vulnerability and emotions). In Terrence's story, his father's physical abuse against his mother is an example of violence fueled through patriarchy. And the fact that Terrence turned to numbing out his emotions as a coping tool rather than express his more vulnerable feelings was likely due to this burden of patriarchy (and the burden of racism—since he's already feeling vulnerable living in a Black body, why face that vulnerability in other spaces?). Think about how patriarchy is reflected in your family.

Materialism: Materialism is the obsession with material wealth and the consumption of physical goods over the nurturing of relationships or real self-care. It tends to come from the implicit belief that visibly having "more" equates to increased power and worth.

As someone of the global majority, you're specifically vulnerable to this cultural legacy burden if you've grown up in poverty, learning that scarcity is scary and threatening. If you're like me, you might find yourself seeking out the instant gratification of things, or ownership of possessions in excess, to try to soothe your painful memories of not having enough. And then there's the feeling of sadness, fear, or anger when you don't have enough money and cannot afford to buy the necessities to help your family. You likely compare yourself to others who have what you lack, and end up feeling like you don't measure up. You might find yourself trying to miti-gate the fear and insecurity that being a Black, Indigenous, and Person of Color living with minimal means can cause. Perhaps you compensate for it with materials, telling yourself this makes you "good" or "complete." Thing is, you're born with everything you need on the inside. So the feeling of lack or void within comes from the message of the larger system that says you aren't enough or whole.

Individualism: Individualism is the belief that we have to entirely focus on ourselves over partners, family members, friends, and members of our com-munity. It encourages and favors self-reliance and independence over col-lective collaboration and healing. Particularly in American culture, it serves to further isolate and separate us, as folks of the global majority, from the healing resources and support provided by close relationships, healthy and functional family units, ancestral practices, and strong com-munity ties.

This isn't to say that self-reliance or independence is "bad" or wrong"—just that when we disregard others and only worry about ourselves, we perpetuate individualism. The goal is a balance between independence (self-reliance) and codependence (heavy reliance on others), which is called *interdependence*. Interdependence encourages us to care for ourselves individually, as well as to care for our communities through group healing.

I believe that messages from cultural legacy burdens can inform a family's legacy burdens and can eventually trickle down to worsen personal burdens. As you can see in figure 2, cultural legacy burdens can create the legacy burdens in your family when they're woven into family messages and parenting beliefs influenced by these cultural burdens. Moreover, cultural legacy burdens can influence how you see yourself, the ways in which you move through your life, and your process of healing as you begin to recover from the grief and traumatic stress they cause. All the while, your day-to-day experiences with systemic and interpersonal racism continue to intensify the personal burdens you face.

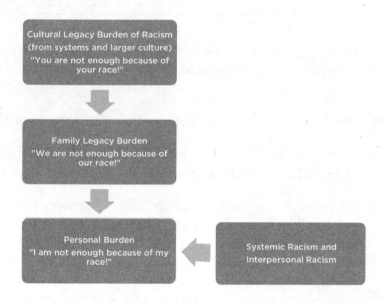

Figure 2: The impact of cultural legacy burdens.

As a Black, Indigenous, and Person of Color, it's important for you to explore and understand how cultural legacy burdens impact the rest of the burdens you carry. They can show up in the stories you tell yourself about yourself even without your knowledge, such as:

- when you believe you're an imposter in school or at work because of your race

- when you're afraid to speak up in predominantly White spaces

- when you're policing your tone, your appearance, and that of others

- when you're uncomfortable feeling joy because you're waiting for it to be stolen from you again

- when you believe (or have been told by family) you need to work harder than others to prove your worth

- when you're encouraged by family to partner with White bodies to "improve the race"

- when you're finding yourself heavily competing with others, even friends, because of a deep-rooted fear that there isn't enough for everyone

- when you're convincing yourself you don't belong at that table

- when you're not able to save money because materialism has you trying to keep up with the Joneses

- when you discourage your children from liking certain colors or toys based on their assigned sex and assumed gender

These are just a few examples of many. Can you already see how these cultural legacy burdens have negatively affected your life? Are you starting to get a sense of how these cultural burdens were woven into your family's legacy burdens, passed down as messages and family patterns, and disguised as a cultural norm? And how this has led to more disconnection and intergenerational trauma? Here is a meditation practice I offer you as an invitation for you to go inward to explore your personal experiences with cultural legacy burdens and how they appear in your life.

MEDITATION PRACTICE:
Connecting to Legacy Burdens

(You can download an audio recording of this practice at http://www.newharbinger.com/49319.)

If it feels right, begin taking deep breaths as you turn your attention inside...each breath creating more and more relaxation in your body. Notice your body softening, your muscles releasing tension, and your heart opening. Allow your mind, body, and heart to expand. Notice the openness. Notice the spaciousness.

Step 1: When you're ready, think about the legacy burdens you carry—those deeply rooted inherited beliefs you have about yourself or the world that really aren't yours...maybe you're aware of pain passed down in your lineage that seems much bigger than you...or maybe you've noticed your life impacted by cultural legacy burdens like racism, individualism, materialism, patriarchy, sexism, homophobia, transphobia, sizeism, ableism, and other isms...and maybe these cultural legacy burdens have informed how you and your family show up in the world. Take a moment to just notice what you carry.

Step 2: See what feels like yours and what may belong to those who came long before you, also reflecting on what might belong to the larger system that we've all grown up in that has taken from you. Ask yourself: *What percentage of the burdens I carry are mine, and what percentage of these burdens are family or cultural legacy burdens?* Just notice. You don't have to change anything about what you see right now.

Step 3: As you prepare to transition back into the space you're in, take a couple of deep breaths...each exhale bringing you one step closer to the outside world. When you're back, and if it feels sincere, extend gratitude to yourself for showing up how you did. Give yourself a moment, and then begin to shift into a space for writing.

JOURNALING PRACTICE:
Describing the Burdens in Your Own Life

Step 1: In your notebook, devote a page to your personal experiences with each type of family legacy burden and cultural legacy burden—plus others if you wish—so you can refer back to them as you continue reading. As a reminder, these are just four of many cultural legacy burdens that can create family legacy burdens. Include a page for:

- Racism (struggling with your own internalized racism, using anti-Black language and stereotypes, claiming that you don't see color)

- Patriarchy (boys [assigned male at birth] receiving preference and favor in the family over the girls [assigned female at birth], homophobia, transphobia)

- Materialism (self-soothing through retail therapy, compulsive spending when bored)

- Individualism (always fending for yourself, hoarding resources and not considering others)

- Other ism

Step 2: After you've written down your personal experiences with racism, patriarchy, materialism, individualism, and/or other isms, pause, reflect, and then write down the answers to these questions:

- What cultural legacy burdens do I carry? (*Examples: implicit bias from anti-Blackness, hoarding resources in excess when others around you need them, absorbed negative beliefs against your marginalized identities—like when you've internalized racism or oppression*)

- Which cultural legacy burdens have I perpetuated? (*Examples: mistreating others because of their marginalized identity, judging people because of their body size [i.e., sizeism], refusing to honor people's pronouns, looking down on others who have less than you, tone policing, ableism*)

- What legacies of historical trauma are in my family? (*Examples: land theft, enslavement, genocide, war and famine, colonization*)

- What legacy burdens come from the historical trauma in my lineage? (*Examples: constant worry of mortality, learned help-lessness and voicelessness, fear of scarcity, using violence to teach obedience in children, fear of rest, discouraging crying or any show of vulnerability because you have to be strong, parents regularly withholding affection, yelling and screaming during conflict*)

- What personal burdens do I have? (*Examples: sexual trauma in childhood or adulthood, homelessness, physical assault, physical and emotional neglect, being bullied in school*)

- How would I be different if I weren't carrying all these burdens? (*Examples: more confident, free to be myself, less people pleasing, comfortable giving or receiving love*)

- Would releasing these burdens create more space in my heart for my family and culture?

By writing responses to these questions, you will gain language and context surrounding the cultural legacy burdens in your past and present. This will help you talk about it, share your feelings, and see situations more clearly for what they are. It will also offer you the opportunity to take responsibility for any burdens you may have inadvertently perpetuated yourself, empowering you to make different choices in the future.

Healing always begins with awareness and recognition of (at times painful) truths so that you can be more aware of how you might be hurting others, and yourself, without even knowing it. Now that you're seeing your own experience more clearly, let's look at how these burdens were placed on you.

How the Cultural Burden of Racism Is Transmitted

It's clear that the moment you come into this world in a Black or Brown body, you're surrounded by racism that can cause grief and traumatic stress. And as a person of the global majority, you're born into the world with some burdened energy in your body and mind from the historical trauma in your ancestral lineages. And whether you know it or not, you're also born with a core Self that holds powerful energy and qualities of who you really are, unburdened.

There are three main ways that the cultural legacy burden of racism is passed down in our communities: in the body before birth, during childhood, and through the environment. These three channels are responsible for the transmission of the painful beliefs your heart has absorbed from the larger culture, and the legacy burdens of your family, which came from historical trauma and systemic racism and oppression today. Let's examine these three means of transmission.

In the body before birth: Because trauma has the ability to change the way your genes are expressed, it can also alter the genes of all future generations born afterward. Prolonged exposure to trauma leads to an increased production of stress hormones and chemicals needed for survival. Trauma over time can also lead to changes in a person's genes. And genetic shifts can continue to be passed down throughout the generations.

For example, consider the effects of the cultural legacy burden of racism endured by someone in a Black or Brown body carrying a fetus in the womb. Trauma is passed down through what is called *in-utero exposure*. If you're an expectant parent enduring physical violence by your partner, the child forming in your womb is at risk for developing genetic and physiological differences, same as if you'd been inhaling cigarette smoke every day of your pregnancy.

This in-utero exposure can affect more than one generation. Did you know that a fetus in the womb with ovaries already has all the eggs it will ever produce? Just as that fetus can have genetic and physiological changes in-utero, the genes in the eggs of that fetus can also be changed by stressors in the womb. It's mind-blowing to think that three generations—the expectant parent, the fetus, and the eggs in that fetus's ovaries—can be genetically altered by stressors during the pregnancy. By understanding this, you can see that both cultural and family legacy burdens are not just beliefs; they're also physically expressed. *Legacy burdens are cyclical, transferred through ancestral lines, and informed by historical trauma.*

The traumas that your ancestors directly experienced can inform and affect *your* genes and physiology, resulting in more vulnerability to mental health struggles like depression and anxiety, a compromised immune system and higher instances of disease, and even higher susceptibility to posttraumatic stress as you grow.[3]

During childhood: Trauma that occurred in childhood, or developmental trauma, may have shaped and influenced your struggle with CPTSD later in life. These early traumatic experiences—perhaps emotional abuse, emotional neglect, abandonment, or physical violence—may also have led to severed relationships between you and your parents or caregivers.

You might find that your caregivers struggled with their *own* legacy burdens, forms of oppression, and racial trauma as they raised you. They may have parented you in ways that were (intentionally or not) abusive, neglectful, and hurtful and led to long-term grief, attachment issues (difficulties forming secure, stable relationships with others), and vulnerability to abuse from others. They may have burdened you with painful things they said, or hurt you with what they didn't say. And in adulthood, you might have found yourself still burdened by the painful energy of these beliefs, sometimes perpetuating the same burden onto others.

Through the environment: As you know, living in an environment that's racist, discriminatory, and oppressive is traumatizing and forges beliefs about you (burdens) that aren't yours. And your body reacts. Your human body is designed to detect threat and activate a fight-or-flight response in order to survive, but the problem arises when you're *constantly* in a threatening environment due to racism, which means your body is almost always in survival mode.

That exhaustion you feel out of nowhere is a sign. Racism doesn't allow you to fully live and be yourself, so when you're burdened by a racist environment, your body will do whatever it needs to get temporary rest from the pain. Some of your coping behaviors might be judged as unhealthy on the outside. But I believe all of them, as scary as they might look and feel, are ways you're trying to soothe unhealed pain inside your burdened inner world. These attempts at survival are trailheads that lead to your inside world. Your coping behaviors show you what needs witnessing, caring for, and unburdening. If we can just approach them with curiosity and compassion, we might find what is underneath it all. These attempts at coping or survival may look like:

- explosive rage or panic attacks

- substance use to "numb" the fear and anger

- chronic muscle tension, injury, and illness

- self-harm behaviors

- full-blown *dissociation* (disconnecting from one's body and surroundings because a situation is too overwhelming)

Take a moment here to pause and ask yourself how you react when you're feeling scared, angry, sad, and hurt. It can be about anything, not just racial trauma. Can you relate to any of these survival strategies? Write about your experience in your notebook.

To Wrap It All Up...

Michelle Obama once said racism changes the shape of your soul. That really hit me deep. Our mental health field tends to understand CPTSD as being the result of prolonged or repeated relational trauma from caregivers or partners or extended exposure to violence, such as in war situations. However, I've found from my Black and Brown clients, my lived experience, and the many lived experiences of the Black and Brown folks around me that racial trauma and oppression also lead to CPTSD. This happens because of the pervasive impact of present-day systemic racism *and* its perpetuation of cultural legacy burdens. These have a ripple effect that creates the legacy burdens in our families and deepens our own wounds.

Your suffering is complex and multilayered; it spans generations, weaving itself into the very genetic makeup of your family in the past up until now. I wholeheartedly believe we cannot fully understand complex trauma if we're dismissing cultural legacy burdens and the grave impacts of racism, oppression, and marginalization. These, too, are relational—they disrupt your relationship to your community, your trust in your Self, and your trust in the world.

Racism attempts to violate your soul. It interrupts your life and you might find yourself silencing your voice and numbing out—exiling your pain to where *you* can't even see it. So much happens underneath the surface in our bodies that has been happening for many generations.

So now that we've journeyed into exploring cultural legacy burdens and how they show up in your life, many times unconsciously, let's go deeper into how racial trauma and the trauma of cultural legacy burdens show up in your body (and brain). It's time to begin practicing the first step of the cultural empowerment approach to healing—using your body to regulate your own well-being. Familiarizing yourself with your body's response to threat, and being able to slow yourself down when feeling overwhelmed, is vital to accessing the parts of your brain that help you thrive. Please take care of yourself in the ways that you need right now. I'm sending so much love to you.

CHAPTER 3

First Empowerment Step: Use Your Body to Regulate Your Own Well-Being

First, I just want to say, if you're a person with racialized and marginalized identities carrying lineages of pain and one who has experienced suffering in this lifetime, you might struggle with connecting with, loving, and seeing your body. If this is you, it makes entire sense to me why you might hide from your body. Many of us go about our days with our heart racing, our muscles tense, and our jaws clenched so hard it's as if we are holding our breaths and words in captivity and we don't even know it. I've met with survivors of sexual trauma, racial trauma, and transphobia who've shared having complicated feelings toward their body, some feeling disgust because the world taught them to hate it and because paying attention to the body was a reminder of the time(s) someone abused it. It might feel counterintuitive to focus on what's happening inside you when you've been taught to hate your body, or if your body carries the emotional and physical scars of being violated.

Naturally, there might be parts of you that avoid connection to your body. I get that, and I want to make space for all the feelings that come up for you around your body. Your ambivalence, reluctance, and open heart are welcome to journey with you throughout this work. Especially because any ambivalence or reluctance you feel is only trying to protect you. I believe your resistance has your best interest at heart when it works so hard to help you survive a world that hurts you. And you might also have a hard time trusting—others and yourself. Take your time with this, and go at your own pace. One thing though, I promise you that your body (a.k.a. the vessel that stores all your stories and feelings) has so many important things to say to you. Are you willing to take the risk and listen?

Take a moment to pause right now and ask yourself these questions. You're welcome to write them down in your journal.

- Do I hide from my body?

- How do I treat my body?

- How do I see my body?

- How does my body tell me I feel safe?

- How does my body tell me I feel threatened?

If you're someone of the global majority, then you've probably felt the world force its racist structures and beliefs onto you, and you might even find yourself afraid to live in your own body. Your painful past and current stressors from living in a structurally racist and oppressive system may have shifted your nervous system's default from a grounded and calm state—one in which your body feels peace and tranquility—to one of hypervigilance, numbness, or tension.

Reclaiming your relationship to your body is one of the most important gifts to give yourself, especially in a world that has taught you to hate your body as a result of internalized racism, sizeism, sexism, ableism, transphobia, and other relational wounding. *Being fluent in your body's language is the antidote to trauma.* So much has happened underneath the surface in your body and brain that has brewed for generations. Witnessing your pain and connecting to your inner world creates space for love and self-compassion.

This first empowerment step involves *self-regulation*, or perhaps more accurately, *co-regulation*. While these exercises encourage self-regulation (or a calming of your body led by you), I believe these processes are truly co-regulation. Because we are not alone when we're taking a walk in nature or sitting in the park. We aren't alone when we're meditating near our family pets. When we are grounding and calming our bodies, we are using our senses, borrowing from nature and the world around us. We are present with the energies surrounding us, with Earth's elements, and with our ancestors within. We are never really doing this work alone.

To benefit from this step, try the practices I offer in this chapter to make a connection with your body. Then you will be able to do a one- to two-second intentional relaxation of your muscles dozens or hundreds of times a day. Calming your body in the moment is brief and can be done anywhere you want—or need—to do it.

In this chapter, I've included three of my favorite practices from Dr. Eric Gentry's *Forward-Facing Trauma Therapy*: the body scan, pelvic floor relaxation, and deep belly breathing. In addition are my offerings of guided practices for you to deeply and intentionally explore your inner world of feelings and parts. As a reminder, not every practice will resonate with you, and that's okay. I invite you to have compassion for yourself when things come up, when it feels rough, and work with any shame or perceived threats you feel in your body. I also encourage carving out some time in your day for stillness—quiet reflection in a place where you feel comfortable to reflect and deepen the connection to your inner world and body.

MEDITATION PRACTICE:
The Body Scan, or "Wet Noodle"

(You can download an audio recording of this practice at
http://www.newharbinger.com/49319.)

Let's gently start by connecting with sensations. Try scanning your body and practice relaxing into a "wet noodle"—without muscle tension, floppy and flexible.

Step 1: Sit or lie comfortably in a place of your choice. Take a deep breath in, and a long and slow breath out, pacing your exhale. Make sure your exhale is longer than your inhale as the out-breath is what is essential to relax. You will soon learn how doing this slows down your heart rate and activates your parasympathetic nervous system.

Step 2: Visualize a healing light (this can be your favorite color/color combo) scanning your body, starting from the top of your head. Scan the top of your head, your forehead, and move down toward your nose and down toward your jaw. Release any tension you notice in these areas.

Step 3: Continue scanning, next your neck muscles, your throat, and your shoulders. Notice any tension as the scan moves through these areas. Take a deep breath and release tension with your exhale.

Scan down to your chest, your heart, down to your stomach. Notice any tension in these areas and release it as you exhale.

Then scan to your arms, wrists, to the tips of your fingers. Take a deep breath in and release the tension from these parts of your body in your exhale breath.

Scan down to your pelvis area. Pay special attention to the energy area between your belly button, hips, and rectum. This emotional center of the pelvis can be the storage for old survival stories. Breathe in, and give a slow and long exhale as you release the tension in your pelvis and private areas.

Continue to move farther down to your thighs, knees, shin, calves, ankles, and toes. Notice any tension residing in your muscles.

Step 4: Take a deep breath in, and a long and slow exhale out. As you exhale, release the tension stored in these areas. Rest.

Step 5: As you rest, check in with yourself. Notice the relaxation in your body. How does your body feel? Is there any more tension left? If so, go back to where this tension is and take another deep breath in. Ask that place in your body what it wants you to know about it. Listen to the message your body's tension has for you. When you're ready, and as you exhale, feel the tension softening, or leaving your body. Repeat this exercise as often as you need.

If you find yourself feeling tearful as you complete this exercise, it makes sense. You've gone through so much. Please allow yourself to see your grief. To feel your sadness. Sometimes what is needed in the moment is for us to make room for our deep emotions. When you make room for your feelings to come to the surface, you can lean into them and give them care and compassion. You're creating a safe body for yourself in the moment when you allow for your emotions to have a space, a witness, and a voice.

Now that you have a taste of the first empowerment step, I'd like to give you a deeper understanding about what's going on in your brain and body beneath your awareness that the exercises aim to help you develop. Some parts of you might want to bypass this brain/body section, but try to stick it through. Becoming familiar with how your nervous system operates can shed light on your own inner system so that you understand what these processes feel and look like for you when you're experiencing racial trauma and other painful experiences. Healing is all about creating new neural pathways in the brain to help you respond differently to perceived threats around you. This happens through awareness, practice, and receiving care from people in your community.

Trying to Survive for Too Long

The good news is that your body has the answers. It knows exactly how to heal itself, and your mind knows how to help you survive. In fact, your mind and body have collaboratively created an intricate system that informs you of when you might be in danger so that you can attempt to overcome a threat or escape it. Way before you're even conscious of how you're feeling, your body has already begun picking up cues of safety or danger in your environment, a process called *neuroception*. (I'll say more on neuroception later in this chapter.) If your body is perceiving threat, it prompts your brain's hypothalamus and hormone glands to release stress hormones and chemicals to help you save yourself. This process is a natural response to threat, your brain and body's evolutionary drive for survival.

Your body is behaving as it's meant to. The problem becomes when you're facing racism every day, or you're on heightened alert anticipating the daily dose of racism (even that subtle kind, where an experience leaves you doubting your intuition, wondering if someone's words or actions were racist and trying to rationalize it away), and your brain and body are releasing these hormones (like cortisol) and chemicals (like norepinephrine) in excess for long periods of time.

If this is your experience, your nervous system remains in an *activated state* for a prolonged period of time and, too often, this creates an expectation and pattern for your nervous system to have more charged energy. And if you're in this state for too long, you might begin withdrawing and shutting down to cope even more. In that *shutdown state*, you might feel numb or resigned. When you're in these states long enough, and regularly, you might mistake being hypervigilant (like anxious) or being shut down for your personality. But it's really that you're habitually stuck living your life in a body hurting from traumatic stress. As I teach you how to self-regulate, let's look at what's happening in your body that makes calming it so important.

When you regulate your body, you're restoring clarity in your inner world. You're slowing down, relaxing into a calm, grounded body. To relax your body is to also calm your mind. A calm mind can help you have more clarity and can help you focus, connect, reason, and be more intentional about your choices. That's because when you're calm, you're likely to be using your prefrontal cortex—the part of your brain responsible for insight, impulse control, compassion, emotion, and body regulation. Your prefrontal cortex (particularly your hippocampus) calms the emotion-centered part of your brain called the *amygdala*, which holds your painful traumatic memories and fires up when you're feeling fear or anger. You can learn to regulate your body while deactivating your stress response so you can relax and feel calm, grounded, and restored. One way to do this is through breathwork, as your breath connects your outer world to your inner world. Let's try it.

MEDITATION PRACTICE:
Deep Belly Breathing

(You can download an audio recording of this practice at http://www.newharbinger.com/49319.)

As newborns, we were born knowing how to breathe most effectively. If you look at how an infant breathes, you will see their belly rise and fall. Children breathe with their diaphragms when they're born and for much of their early lives. It isn't until they've had enough lived experience that they shift the way they take in air. As we grow, we begin to breathe solely from our chests and lift our shoulders while we're inhaling, resulting in less air inhaled. Much of this is due to the busy lives we find ourselves living, where we are often on the go, and our breathing is shallow and constricted. We might also be activated by others throughout the day, which negatively impacts our breathing. Naturally, when our breath is constricted, our mind and body signal danger to one another. Taking deep, restorative breaths is a necessary and proven way to reintroduce calm, grounding, and a sense of some safety back into your body.

Step 1: To start, sit comfortably wherever you choose and relax your neck, shoulders, and back. Locate your diaphragm by placing one hand below your rib cage and the other on the upper part of your chest. Alternatively, you can also place both hands behind your neck or above your head and watch your diaphragm rising and falling as it fills with air and releases.

Step 2: Slowly breathe in for five seconds through your nose and watch your stomach rise as your diaphragm takes in your breath. Notice the sensation of your lungs filling with air. Try to keep the upper part of your chest as still as possible as you're breathing.

Step 3: As you exhale, watch your stomach falling and releasing the air. The goal is for you to have more practice with belly breaths than with shallow breathing from your upper chest. Breathing with our diaphragms is how we take in full breaths.

Step 4: Repeat this 1–5 times for five minutes and as needed. Notice how you feel in your body. Deep belly breathing is truly one of the most important and basic practices. Breath gives us life.

Step 5 (optional): As you are taking deep belly breaths, slowly breathe in for five seconds. As you slowly exhale, softly sing the word *home*. Then *love*. Do this for one to five minutes. Allow your spirit to lead you to create an inner vibration and to sing yourself back home into your body.

Your breath works with your nervous system and reminds you that you're safely living in *this present moment*. Breath work is necessary for you because breathing deeply and intentionally can help stop the trauma response in our bodies. As I'll now share, living in a prolonged state of a fight-or-flight trauma response in the body creates long-term medical issues for us, and often for future generations.

Learning to Relax Your Trauma Response

Living in activated (hyperaroused) or shutdown (hypoaroused) states when you're in survival mode in your environment has long-term consequences for your health, including increased risk of autoimmune issues, diabetes, and cardiovascular disease.[4] Racism and oppression are monstrosities that create emotional, psychological, and physiological distress and put you in survival mode way longer than what is healthy for your autonomic nervous system—whether you're activated or shut down. Let's talk more about that for a moment. You might be asking yourself, what is the autonomic nervous system and what does it have to do with traumatic stress? Well...

Your autonomic nervous system is in charge of everything your body does, whether you consciously know it or not. It regulates your blood pressure and breathing rate. It controls the internal body processes for your heart, blood sugar, blood vessels, lungs, digestive system, body temperature, and a lot more. As your autonomic nervous system perceives signals of threat to your body from the environment, it responds by activating either your sympathetic nervous system (fight or flight) or parasympathetic nervous system (freeze or shut down), which prepare you to either fight, run away, freeze, or numb out depending on what coping strategies are needed in that moment.

Sympathetic Nervous System

The sympathetic nervous system (SNS) is the component of your autonomic nervous system that activates the fight-or-flight response. It's in charge of preparing you to fight what you're perceiving as a threat or mobilizing you to run away—for instance, if you're walking at night by yourself and someone approaches closely behind you, or if you're pulled over by the police. In this state, you might first notice your heart beginning to race, and you might begin sweating or breathing faster. Your nervous energy comes from the SNS, so anxious or intense energy is usually a signal that you're perceiving threat and are hyperaroused. Behaviorally, you might cope in this state with rapid speech, restlessness, yelling, or throwing things, and you might have difficulty relaxing or sleeping.

Think of what it takes to drive a car. The SNS is like a car's gas pedal. Your body's activation is like your foot pressing the gas pedal. You're just driving without stopping, sometimes even speeding dangerously unless you hit your brakes to slow the car down—or you crash. If you're up for it, see what it's like for you to be in this state. Ask yourself:

- How does my body tell me that my sympathetic nervous system is activated? (heart starts racing, face gets flushed, get restless)

- What kinds of things do I do when I'm hyperaroused? (scream, break things, have a panic attack)

Now that you have a sense of how you show up with an activated sympathetic nervous system, let's see what it's like for you when your parasympathetic nervous system takes the wheel.

Parasympathetic Nervous System

The parasympathetic nervous system (PNS) acts like the brake of your car. When you're going too fast (SNS), your brakes slow you down. As you step on the PNS brake, and your car slows down, you're able to get more control of your vehicle.

Neuroscientist Dr. Stephen Porges proposed a theory called the *polyvagal theory*, explaining that the parasympathetic nervous system branches into two subsystems.[5] The first one (and oldest evolutionary function) is the *dorsal vagal subsystem*, and the second (and newer evolutionary function) is the *ventral vagal subsystem*. Both subsystems are connected to the vagus nerve, which is the longest cranial nerve and links your brain to your body from your brain stem to your colon. The vagus nerve is essentially the glue of the parasympathetic nervous system. It sends sensory information to your brain and also controls the movement of some of your muscles and the different functions of your glands. It's responsible for monitoring your heart rate and digestion. (This is why the PNS is sometimes called the "rest and digest" system.)

Resmaa Menakem, trauma therapist and author of *My Grandmother's Hands*, refers to the vagus nerve as the *soul nerve* because it is connected to all the processes that help us come alive, connect with others, or disengage.[6]

Let's look at how the polyvagal theory applies to you.

THE CALM STATE

When your ventral vagal subsystem is activated, your PNS is in control. Here you're calm, chill, and thinking clearly. Your heart is open, your cortex is online, and it feels like you're living your best life. Here you may feel more of a sense of connection to yourself and others, so you benefit from returning to this state as often as you can.

THE SHUTDOWN STATE

The flip side to being in a ventral vagal state is being here in dorsal vagal. When you experience a low level of activation in your dorsal vagal state, you can benefit from calming practices, like sleeping and dreaming, digesting your food, meditating, and spending deep reflective moments within. Indigenous practices incorporating ceremonial spiritual medicine (like Ayahuasca, for example) serve to stimulate a dorsal vagal state of dream or trance.

But when your dorsal vagal state is in high activation, you're shut down. Your heart rate is slow, and your breathing is slow, but you aren't calm. Sometimes you end up in this state when you've been in a fight-or-flight response for so long that you begin to feel helpless and shift into your PNS's dorsal vagal shutdown state. Other times, this may just be your go-to coping state—especially if you often struggle with speaking up or being seen and feel hopeless and resigned. When your dorsal vagal state is in high activation, you can fold, freeze, numb out, or dissociate. You can literally faint in this state.

When you're numb and shut down in a dorsal vagal state, you may see yourself as disconnected and empty. But numbness is not a sign of emptiness. It's a sign that you're overwhelmed, like an NYC summer day when you (along with everyone in the city) have your air conditioner blasting and your entire home (or street) experiences a blackout. When too much electricity is running simultaneously, it can become overwhelming and the circuit breaker will shut off the electricity to ensure safety and avoid a fire. Like the circuit breaker, when you're feeling inundated with stress that's toxic and there's a lot going on internally, your brain initiates a shutdown and can dissociate so that all your reserves are aimed toward your survival.

If you're dissociating, you may feel like you're having an out-of-body experience, or losing awareness of the present moment and your surroundings. You might miss your stop on the train because you were lost staring into space. These are just a few examples of mild forms of dissociation, as the severity of dissociation can occur on a continuum from the mild examples I mentioned to a dissociative diagnosis. And if you carry a diagnosis of dissociative identity disorder, I want you to know that this doesn't mean you're damaged. It says you've lived through so much pain growing up that splitting and turning off were the only options to help protect you and to survive it all. And I'm thankful you did all that you could and knew, for survival.

I have so much appreciation for the parts of you and within me that jump in to shut us down when we're feeling cues of danger. Especially living as a Black, Indigenous, and Person of Color, dissociation is all about survival in a world that's inequitable and perpetuates White supremacy and oppression. When you're experiencing extreme and prolonged toxic stress, your brain is going to do what it needs to do to help you survive, and shut down the part of your brain (the prefrontal cortex) that keeps you present and conscious. If you've experienced racial trauma and are a survivor of other traumatic experiences (including as a child), your nervous system is probably really skilled at dissociation—as your brain and body were forced to adapt to help you avoid or survive the harm of your home or the outside world. Staying silent for survival can be a form of dissociating from yourself or the external environment, especially if you struggle being heard in a system that doesn't listen—and if you also felt unheard in your family.

When you really think about it, both your sympathetic and parasympathetic states within the autonomic nervous system play a key role in your protection and healing when they're not in overdrive. You just want to make sure that you're not in these states for too long. If you're willing, explore a typical day and think about what it's like for you to be in a parasympathetic state. Ask yourself:

- How does my body signal to me that I'm in a ventral vagal state? (feeling calm, confident, connected to myself and others)

- How does my body signal to me that I'm in high activation of a dorsal vagal state? (feeling shut down, hopeless, discouraged; having cold extremities)

- What kinds of things do I do when I'm shut down? (avoid socializing, self-injury, can't connect to my feelings)

An experience like enduring microaggressions daily can continually activate your survival response on a regular basis to fight off the threat, escape the threat, or freeze and shut down when you feel powerless over the threat. When your protective coping mechanisms are on overdrive like this, trying to help you get through the day, it can leave you feeling exhausted. But know this:

Coping is not healing. Your coping mechanisms are meant to be temporary and help you tolerate stress; they won't heal you.

Only your higher Self (your soul) connected to the collective soul of your community can help you heal. We'll speak more about your protective parts and the inner wisdom of your higher Self in chapter 5.

When your body or mind feel stressed from experiencing abuse in the form of daily microaggressions, you're perceiving threat in your social environment. The threats are there, but your body cannot distinguish the difference in level of danger between a microaggression and an imminent threat to your physical safety or survival. So when you master your ability to modulate your threat response, or self/co-regulate, and are able to "pause" or "soften" that survival instinct temporarily so that your brain can come back online, you can respond with the appropriate thoughts and behaviors that the specific situation requires. With this process, you're not only healing your body of existing trauma, but you're better equipping yourself to care for your emotions because you have access to your higher brain functions to make the best decisions for yourself, and more space for clarity toward all that you're holding.

Heeding Your Inner Alarm

All of your daily experiences get processed by your brain sequentially.[7] This means that every sound, taste, image, smell, and physical sensation that your body receives from your surroundings enters your brain in a linear sequence to be processed. Everything you experience first goes through the bottom of your brain (the brain stem) for you to process before eventually traveling up to your forebrain and limbic system, which scan for threat and gauge your emotional safety. Dr. Dan Siegel, a psychiatrist and founder of Mindsight, calls the lower, instinctive parts of the brain "the downstairs brain."[8] The lower part of your brain begins to review every one of your experiences, and if it detects any similarities between an issue of today and past wounding, your inner alarm goes off. If by chance something or someone reminds you of any traumatic experience you've had, your fight, flight, freeze, or shutdown coping state kicks in. This then turns off your cortex, the uppermost part of the brain, making it impossible for you to reason, have a good sense of what's happening, or make decisions most aligned with who you really are.

This is why it's so incredibly important to recognize when you're feeling activated or overwhelmed by parts of you carrying pain, because without your even knowing it, your nervous system can shift into an ongoing fight, flight, freeze, or shutdown response and chronically interfere with your quality of life. When this happens, you might find yourself often reacting to people with what Dr. Frank Anderson, a lead internal family systems trainer and psychiatrist, calls "trauma-colored glasses."[9]

If your experience passes the test and doesn't match any past trauma, this feedback goes up to the cortex for processing, which helps you reason, connect, and make choices from a place of awareness. Similarly, if you're able to interrupt your threat response and calm your body, you can turn your cortex back online. Your cortex is considered "the upstairs brain."[10]

Reminding Yourself to Self-Regulate

Imagine you're a parent, tired and overworked. Your toddler continuously follows you around the house, not letting you have a moment of silence for yourself. You begin to scream at your toddler. In that moment, you struggle to have access to compassion because your emotional reserves are depleted and your brain launches a threat response. You need to slow down and relax your body to be able to relate to others with compassion. Only then can you access your ability to choose how you want to respond. From there you will continue emotionally and physically self-regulating, and will connect with your heart space.

Doing this can empower you to exist unapologetically and take up space, even when you're enduring the daily microaggressions. Because at the end of the day, you're creating an inner buffer between you and the vitriol of the outside world that will have less of a grip on your nervous system. Three important words to remember from psychiatrist Dr. Bruce Perry are:

Regulate

Relate

Reason

You can chant these words to yourself like a mantra if it helps you to remember. It's a simple reminder of the sequential process of your brain. That you must (1) regulate your body—and interrupt your threat response—to feel calm and less overwhelmed, in order to (2) deeply relate with others and (3) make decisions you're proud of.

Restoring Your Ability to Rest

Your mind and body have a reciprocal relationship—to hurt one is to hurt both. And one of the ways oppression manifests in Black, Indigenous, and People of Color is in not allowing yourself to rest. Do you remember Terrence's story? One of the messages he learned from his family and the larger system was to avoid rest and always be productive. In my family, my grandfather has always said, "No dejes para mañana lo que se puede hacer hoy," or "Don't leave for tomorrow what can be done today." That comes from a legacy burden to overwork and produce, minimizing the need for rest. But what if rest is really what you're needing instead of completing that task? In fact, that task *could* probably wait until tomorrow.

Rest can feel threatening when life has shown you that letting your guard down leaves you open to more harm. You might wonder how your body can rest in a world that seeks to erase you. How you can rest your body when you're constantly feeling like you don't belong. How you can rest your body with racial trauma. Although you may not be able to permanently eradicate your body's threat response while living within a racist and oppressive system in a Black, Indigenous, or Brown racialized body, it's possible to have moments to restore and protect your body's sacred energy—and in fact, it's vital for the care of your mind, body, and spirit.

So much of our story inhabits the emotional center of the pelvis. We cannot relax if our pelvic area isn't relaxed. The pelvis makes up your survival center. It sometimes carries stories of body violations, sexual abuse, and life-threatening memories. This practice encourages you to continue establishing safety as you work toward reclaiming relaxation in this core area of your body.

MEDITATION PRACTICE:
Pelvic Floor Relaxation

(You can download an audio recording of this practice at http://www.newharbinger.com/49319.)

If you're a survivor of sexual trauma, please know it's not uncommon for survivors of sexual assault or abuse to struggle with relaxing the pelvic area. Please know that your body is yours and is worth reclaiming. You have a right to unapologetically befriend your body and care for it. Take a deep breath as you do this practice, as often as you need to, and remind yourself that in *this moment* you are safe. Please don't rush any parts of you that feel protective and guarded. Practice at your own pace and take your time.

Step 1: Sit down comfortably and place one hand under each side of your bottom. Feel for your sit bones. These two bones mark the lower part of your core.

Step 2: Now, locate and touch the two bony points above your hips, one on each side of your body. These two points are the upper portion of your core.

Step 3: Create a visual image in your mind that connects all the points together, creating an imaginary square. This square is the energy center of your pelvis. Breathe deeply and send air directly into the center of this square while envisioning it expanding.

Step 4: As you exhale, release the tension in this square and feel it leaving your body. Relax the muscles within the square. Give permission to yourself to feel lighter there. Allow yourself the freedom to release the pain you carry in this survival center.

Step 5: Keep repeating this practice until your pelvic area feels fully relaxed. Thank your body for its efforts to create more safety within. Grant yourself compassion when it cannot. We are all a work in progress, trying our best to undo legacies of violence inflicted on the bodies and spirits of our ancestors. Stay the course and keep working at it.

Let me be clear. The practices in this chapter aren't to get you comfortable with oppression. They are to help you attune to your inner world, your bodily sensations, and your feelings, to empower you from within so that you can resist oppressive systems without hurting your own body. And regulating your body helps create more spaciousness within you for more connection with your community.

Calming your body means you will need to go inward and pay attention to what's happening inside so that you're able to connect with the vulnerable feelings you're holding and be able to care for them. This practice is called *interoception*.

Interoception: Sensing Yourself

When you focus inward on what's happening in your body, or practice interoception, you're getting input from inside your body that helps you feel and discern your physical needs. Like when you're able to tell that you're hungry or full, hot or cold, feeling sick, or when you have to use the bathroom. It's mindfulness of the body.

Your body always communicates to you what it needs. Interoception is important to the healing process because it bridges the body and mind. When your body is activated or shut down, you're in survival mode and not quite feeling safety in your own body. You definitely want to be mindful about scanning your body often for tension, pressure, and any anxious energy because, as you learned earlier in this chapter, if your body is tense and your sympathetic nervous system is activated, your prefrontal cortex goes offline. This means that this very important part of your brain, responsible for insight, connection, and good judgment, is impaired when you're in a fight-or-flight state. When you think about it, if you're in a threat response for the majority of your day, how often are you *really* connecting to yourself and others?

Neuroception: Sensing Your Environment

Your body responds to cues of safety or danger in the environment without you even knowing. The instinctive parts of your brain continuously and innately scan for safety or threat in your environment to keep you safe and connected.

For instance, imagine yourself walking in a forest when something falls to the ground. Your heart immediately starts racing and you're breathing faster. Your sympathetic nervous system is activated. Soon, though, you realize it was just a large branch that had fallen from a tree. You're safe. So you begin to slowly calm your body because you realize there's no danger. Your parasympathetic nervous system kicks in now. Your breath and heart rate return to normal. You feel ready to reconnect and continue enjoying the rest of your hike in the forest.

This is an example of how your sympathetic and parasympathetic nervous system states can be activated through neuroception.

Throughout this chapter, you've been practicing how you can move your body into a relaxed state when you find yourself in a threat response. Remember to go at your own pace and that these are offerings for your body and soul. Take what feels right and leave the rest.

Connecting with Your Body to Heal

When was the last time you gifted yourself inner peace? Sometimes inner peace can feel more like a privilege than a right. You're deserving of reconnecting with your inner peace, and it is always within you. Your inner peace is underneath the rage, grief, fear, shame, and anticipatory loss. Many times, we are so consumed with these heavier emotions that we don't realize how nearby we are to peace. The goal isn't to avoid ever feeling uncomfortable feelings, but rather to not be overwhelmed by them so often. We'll now try tapping into inner peace.

This mindfulness practice is helpful in bridging the body and the breath. When we are engaging with our breath and exploring the many creative ways to reintroduce calmness into our spirits and bodies, it can be helpful to add affirmations with our breath. To speak words rooting you back to the present moment, while you're being intentional about your breath, reminds you that you are safe right now. In a world that feels threatening for you living in a Black, Indigenous, or Brown body, in *this moment* you are safe.

MEDITATION PRACTICE:
Breathing in Healing, Breathing out Legacy Burdens

(You can download an audio recording of this practice at http://www.newharbinger.com/49319.)

Step 1: Find a comfortable and quiet place. You can choose to be with your body in any way that feels inviting and safe. Take a deep cleansing breath in. Drop into your body as far as you're willing to go. Exhale slowly.

Step 2: As you take another slow deep breath in, say to yourself, *I breathe in healing.* As you slowly exhale, say to yourself, *I release the cultural burdens I'm holding* (be specific and name them).

Step 3: With each inhale and exhale, allow your heart to open and your chest to create space for warmth and connection. Continue to inhale what you're wishing to give yourself (maybe self-acceptance, confidence, curiosity, peace) and exhale the legacy burdens (and any personal burdens) you wish to release from your body and spirit. You can:

- Inhale the words *I am safe*, exhale the words *I release tension.*

- Inhale the words *I am love*, exhale the words *I'm not worthy*.

- Inhale the words *I matter*, exhale the words *I am broken*.

- Inhale the words *I am whole*, exhale the words *I am empty*.

- Inhale the words *I am powerful*, exhale the words *I am invisible*.

Repeat this for one to five minutes (or longer if you need). Notice how your body feels now.

Step 4 (optional): If it helps, write down the messages you have taken into your body so they can serve as a reminder throughout your day. The messages you tell yourself are so important if you are to record over internalized racism and any self-loathing or self-abandonment you've learned.

If you've lived decades hearing hurtful messages about yourself, it will naturally become your own story about you. Define yourself in ways that are more aligned with who you are without all of the burdens you carry. This is essential in nourishing your spirit and embodying inner peace. Remember that you can return to these messages anytime you need. They are *your* truth.

Our bodies carry so much of our spoken and unspoken story. If we practice enough stillness, we can hear these feelings and be curious about them. We can grow to understand them and their purpose, which is usually for our survival needs. Ever wonder what your rage is trying to tell you? Or that knot in your throat? We've been conditioned to fear these sensations in our bodies and thoughts in our minds, but they hold such valuable information about how we're experiencing the world that's worth listening to. I'd like to share with you this guided meditation to help you tune in to your body's feelings.

MEDITATION PRACTICE:
Attune to Your Body's Feelings

(You can download an audio recording of this practice at
http://www.newharbinger.com/49319.)

Step 1: Sit comfortably on a chair or lie down on your back in a space that offers safety. Scan your body and notice the areas where you feel tension. Breathe into these areas and feel the tension leaving your body. Continue to breathe in slowly and exhale slowly and peacefully. Ask your mind and body to relax.

Step 2: If there's any part of you reluctant to relax, place your hand over your heart. Take a deep breath in and a long, slow exhale out. Remind yourself that you are safe and can go as slow as you need. When you're ready, drop further into relaxation.

Step 3: Witness the thoughts that are free flowing in your mind without trying to judge them or grab them. Just notice. Observe the things you say about yourself and all that's coming up for you in this moment. Don't try to control these thoughts, just bear witness to them. Notice what the thoughts are and how they manifest in your body. Notice what parts of your body respond to these thoughts.

Step 4: Allow yourself to experience the emotions that are coming up from those thoughts. What do you feel about these thoughts? Are you afraid of them? Are you saddened by them? Remember to only *feel* about your thoughts, not judge them or try to change them.

Step 5: Notice where and how the feeling communicates to you in your body. Simply give a compassionate touch to this part of you and acknowledge its presence. If it feels sincere, reassure the part or feeling with the words *I see you and feel you. I'm here. You're not alone. You matter to me.* You don't have to be afraid of feeling your feelings. They tell your story.

Step 6: Tune in to this feeling's message. What does the feeling want to tell you? Why has it come? Lean into its message as you are also mindful of your breath.

Step 7: Is there another loving message you would like to share with this feeling? What would you like someone to have told you growing up when you felt this way? If it feels right, tell yourself these words. Your body speaks of old wounds; your ancestors speak. Cry with yourself if your heart calls for it.

Step 8: When you're ready, thank the feeling for being with you. Know that you can return to connect with this feeling anytime you wish. If you're open, maybe create a plan to visit again to strengthen your connection with this feeling and understand it more as you follow the trail to see where it leads to in your past. Once you're ready, take one last deep breath, followed by a long, slow exhale. Follow your exhale back into the outside world. Open your eyes and notice where you are in time and space.

Step 9: Check in with yourself. How was that for you? If some big feelings came up and you want to journal about them, please do. It's natural to have been taken over by feelings if it has been a while since you've gone inward. It takes courage for people to acknowledge their most vulnerable feelings, especially carrying cultural legacy burdens.

In your work throughout this chapter, you have done so much to turn inward again and create more flowing energy in your body. You have done this by honoring your spirit and continuing to build trust in yourself. You deserve a hug. *Abrazo mariposa,* or the "butterfly hug," was developed for EMDR (eye movement desensitization and reprocessing) therapy.[11] I use a modified form, which can help you feel a closer bond with your vulnerability by feeling your own embrace. How amazing would it be for you to feel satisfied by your own love and comfort? If you're open, try it. You may find this practice helpful as you tend to feelings of vulnerability like shame, sadness, grief, anger, and rage.

LOVING-KINDNESS PRACTICE:
Embrace Yourself in a Hug

(You can download an audio recording of this practice at http://www.newharbinger.com/49319.)

The butterfly hug is an invitation for you to show up for yourself in the many ways your spirit needs, and maybe needed in your younger years. Sometimes we just need a hug from our loved ones and people in our community. It's also an integral part of our healing to give ourselves that support and care we yearn for. Many times, the things we wish we'd receive from others are the things we don't give ourselves. Hugging yourself means that during moments of pain, you have the ability and power to help shift the threat response in your body with your own touch. This practice is simple yet powerful.

Step 1: Cross your hands and make an X shape over your chest. Make sure your fingers touch the top of your shoulders.

Step 2: Take a deep breath in. Feel your own embrace. Be with yourself in this position for as long as you need. Cry with yourself. Laugh with yourself.

Step 3: Tell yourself the words you most need to hear right now. Remind yourself that you are safe right now. Tell yourself that you're there for you. Tell yourself that you won't leave you. Tell yourself that in hugging yourself, you are also embracing your ancestors. You are your ancestors.

If hugging yourself feels too scary, consider what feels like a safe start. Sometimes, people feel more comfortable holding their own hands first. Trauma histories can teach you not to trust yourself, so can internalized racism and oppression, and as a result some people need to build trust in themselves before they begin offering themselves loving touch. This practice is an act of reclaiming your own power to self-soothe and witness your pain while you tend to its hurt. You'll see how it can open you to wholeheartedly love yourself. Radically loving yourself is liberation work.

To Wrap It All Up...

I honor your willingness to be where are you are right now with all this, whether you were able to get through all of the practices, some of them, or none at all. If you're not ready yet, that's completely fine. You will be, at your own time. One thing I've learned about the impact of White supremacist culture is the pressure of urgency to finish everything right away. This book will not perpetuate that message. Your flow is the right timing for you.

It may seem like an uphill battle, but it's very possible to reclaim your body once again. In the midst of oppression, *this* is your resistance. It's possible to courageously rekindle love for your body, or love it for the first time. You are more powerful than you'll ever know.

Now it's time to embody this power by giving yourself the calm body you've always deserved. It's time for self-compassion. Bearing witness and offering compassion to all of your vulnerable parts' fears and wounding helps gradually release all the cultural, familial, and personal burdens you carry within that are covered in shame.

In the chapters ahead, you're going to learn about Maria Alejandra's struggle with CPTSD; expand your understanding of how CPTSD affects your inner world; and deepen your practice of self-compassion, using the lens of internal family systems therapy, to help you become your own witness and champion using the potent power of your loving Self.

PART II

Toxic Stress Creates Deep Wounds

When you've lived entire decades in survival mode, it's hard to know who you really are. Your ways of coping become how you see yourself. We can find ourselves in a constant state of hypervigilance, feeling anxious and wanting to control circumstances, people, or things. If this sounds familiar, it might lead you to believe you're controlling and anxious. Or if you find yourself shut down and guarded, you might tell yourself that you're stand-offish, uncaring, or cold (maybe others have even described you this way). Earlier I mentioned that if you're living in activated or shutdown nervous system states for too long, you can conflate the sensations in your body, the burdens you carry, and your coping mechanisms with your personality. *But you are not the burdens you're carrying.* When you've carried them long enough, though, you might believe they're who you are. I invite you to ask yourself:

- Who would I be if I weren't carrying the messages I've internalized from the outside world?

- What does my liberation look and feel like?

- What would I be doing differently if I felt safe?

Explore this in your journal. Like you, I'm still working toward my liberation. I remain a work in progress. At my core, I believe I'm playful, courageous, and trusting of others. I'm trying to live my life authentically, connect with people, and love hard on this Earth. I'm also trying to heal with my ancestors—and if I'm really lucky, touch hearts like yours. A fully unburdened inner world of mine would allow me to be unafraid of my voice, take the risk to be vulnerable, and allow people to get closer to me rather than love at a distance.

Can you relate? If you can, even a little, like me you've probably found yourself feeling guarded with people in all kinds of relationships because your past experiences showed you that relationships hurt. You may carry the personal burdens of betrayal from relationships and the added cultural legacy burdens of systemic racism from institutions that betrayed you and your people.

Feeling betrayed by a system designed to oppress and create dispirited-ness in Black, Indigenous, and Brown bodies will naturally hurt deeply. It makes total sense to me if you struggle trusting institutions after experiencing abuse, exploitation, and violence from them. When you feel like they've never even tried to love you. Or to have compassion for your strife. I know this book is dedicated to your racialized identity, and that you will also have other intersecting identities—some that are also marginalized. Know that the following is true for your other identities too: you need to know that *you didn't cause your pain.*

Many of us are traumatized because of the betrayal, abuse, mockery, and invalidation of our pain. Sometimes you're wounded by the people around you, the institutions you're a part of, or the governing laws and "justice" system. I've written "justice" in quotes because oftentimes Black, Indigenous, and People of Color experience more injustice and criminalization than those with White bodies, especially as Black, Latine, and Indigenous groups have the highest rates of incarceration in the US.

If you're not feeling loved, and lovable, you're not alone. It's hard to feel entirely lovable when you're carrying so much shame inside you dealing with *toxic stress* (prolonged adversity creating and accumulating burdens that impact your mind, body, and spirit). Like when you are often racially profiled or called racial slurs; experience daily homophobia, transphobia, and discrimination; or were consistently abused in your home as a child. And sadly, this is not an exhaustive list of what toxic stress is or all you've faced in your life. As an immigrant or refugee, there's toxic stress in your story that led your elders (or yourself) to flee war, poverty, and danger in their (or your) country, only to be met with hate. Abuse. Exploitation. Your very life dismissed by others.

Like our Black siblings, stolen from their ancestral lands of Africa to be enslaved all around the world. Many left without a trace of ancestry because of this genocide and enslavement of Black bodies, to apartheid, to segregation in the US and beyond. And may we never forget the Native Americans indigenous to their ancestral land we now occupy, whose land was stolen and lives taken by genocide and colonization. And who still carry the burdens of this historical trauma and today's struggle to preserve their land, tribes, and mental and physical health.

Racism is toxic stress. Homophobia is toxic stress. Transphobia is toxic stress. Ableism is toxic stress. Sexism is toxic stress. Hate crimes are toxic stress. Immigrant families separated at the border is toxic stress. Isms are toxic stress. They keep going and they keep hurting. They're in the air and filtered in the systems you wake up to every day. And even then, toxic stress is not only your painful present-day experiences (or your childhood trauma), but also the historical trauma of your ancestors still alive in your wounding, creating the long-lasting effects of intergenerational trauma in your family. And your wounds run deep.

Feeling unloved and "othered" creates so much toxic stress on the mind, body, and spirit. You carry the pain of loneliness when you aren't loved. And that pain births shame and may say to you that you aren't lovable or good enough, sometimes because of the way you look and your identities. The world's lies become your own.

So, who's loving you? Who's reminding you of your worthiness? Who sees and accepts you for all of you? *Are you loving you?*

As you move into chapter 4, I'd like you to start thinking about patterns of violence, abuse and neglect, addiction, and health issues passed down in your family. What's the story before your story? Let's read about Maria Alejandra's.

Maria Alejandra's Story (she/her)

Maria Alejandra (nicknamed "Ale") is the nineteen-year-old daughter of undocumented Mexican immigrants who grew up in San Antonio, Texas. She and her two younger siblings witnessed intimate partner violence in their home from birth, when their father would hit their mother. After he passed away from cancer when Ale was seven and her younger siblings were four and two, Ale's mother, Juana, raised them as a single mom.

Juana's parenting style was strict and abusive—she often hit Ale and her siblings with a belt and regularly screamed at Ale. Ale learned at an early age to dissociate and escape her body mentally to deal with the pain of being hit by her mother. If Ale cried from the pain of her physical abuse, Juana would warn her that she'd *really* give Ale something to cry about, and that kids were meant to be seen, not heard.

What confused Ale the most as a kid was that when her mom would hit her or throw things at her, Juana would say she was "doing it because she loved her." Juana would often say that she treated Ale like her own mother had treated her, and that she turned out alright. The only time Juana paid much attention to Ale was when she was calling her names, criticizing her, or hitting her, while the rest of the time Juana expected Ale and her siblings to stay out of the way. This dismissal caused an aching pain inside Ale that never went away, as she learned that the only way she could get the attention of someone she loved was when she did "bad" things.

As Ale grew into her teenage years, she started experiencing her own bouts of rage, and found herself drawn to older guys who were abusive and emotionally unavailable, just like her parents had been. Ale felt emotionally detached in all of her relationships except with her two siblings, whom she felt *too* much responsibility for and protective of.

I want to check in before you read further. How's your heart feeling right now? If you need to take a pause and a breather, please do that. This can be a perfect opportunity to practice interoception and scan your body for any sign of perceived threat, especially if Ale's story resonates with yours. Take some intentional breaths. Remind yourself that whatever you're feeling in this moment is valid. And that, right now, you're safe. What would you want someone to tell you in this moment? If it feels right, offer those very words to yourself. When you're ready to dive in further, keep reading.

Shared Experience: When Wounds Become Complex Posttraumatic Stress

Children exposed to ongoing toxic stress—like emotional or physical abuse, emotional or physical neglect, and violence in the home—are forced to choose survival over their childhood. And Children of Color live with the added stress of racism and less access to educational resources and health care. And, overall, less access to the compassion of others. If you were a child who witnessed abuse in the home, and were abused yourself, you've had to make a trade. You've been forced to trade your peace for hypervigilance and sadness. You've been forced to surrender your innocence for responsibility and to be a *parentified child*.

A parentified child is a child who needs to mature faster to care for their parents (or for themselves), sometimes to protect a parent who's being abused when there's violence in the home, other times to help their parents navigate an oppressive system. For instance, you may have been expected to miss school to attend your parents' appointments and help with paperwork and translation because there wasn't enough help to support your non-English-speaking parents. Or you may have been triangulated between your parents, put in the middle of their arguments and forced to choose a side or be their negotiator, or blamed for their fights. Maybe you've had an experience similar to Ale's, caring for your younger siblings while being a kid yourself—because your parent was in an abusive relationship or was a single parent struggling alone and carrying their own pain and legacy burdens.

If you grew up in an abusive home, you were likely parentified, and burdens were placed on you that shouldn't have been. And this was likely how intergenerational trauma manifested in your family. I'm going to speak more about intergenerational and attachment trauma in chapter 8, but I'd be remiss not to mention it until then because a major part of your family's suffering is informed by historical trauma.

Ale was mostly ignored, and only seen by her mom when she was "bad." When children's mistakes are what guarantee attention from their caregivers, many children will continue to act out in ways that attract negative attention, because it still means being seen and noticed. Even if the love and attention hurts. If you experienced this, you'll understand the sense that bad love is better than no love at all. And this is where shame comes in. Because as a child, you're unable to understand why your parents are hurting you, and will turn your anger inward and blame yourself.

When Ale was being hit by her mother, she would often mentally leave her body. Children who are physically hurt are not only forced to mature quickly, but also need to strategically create safety inside themselves the only way they know how—often through dissociation. Ale would eventually learn to become stoic and not cry, as having tender emotions after being hit was met with more punishment. Her vulnerability was rejected and exiled.

Reflection

Does all this sound familiar to you? I've struggled for so much of my life with giving myself permission to be vulnerable, to have feelings and to share them openly with others without fearing judgment or shame. Shame is so embedded in our wounds when we've been taught to shrink ourselves or disappear. Where there's shame, there is also rage. And rage is grief work, according to Ann Sinko, lead trainer of internal family systems therapy.[12]

I strongly believe that when we don't own our own struggle with traumatic stress (ours and that of society), we can't see the trauma in others. How can we when we turn away from our own? How can you fully understand the struggle of your children when you deny your own? How can you expect to be comfortable with another person's vulnerability when you're not comfortable with your own? This is part of our individual and collective work: becoming more aware of the burdens we carry, so that we can learn to offer love and compassion to all our feelings and parts of us, to then be able to offer that same compassion to others with similar parts and struggles. It's my hope that this book is contributing.

To return to Ale's story and what it reveals, when you witness violence in your home, and when you're hit in the name of love, you learn that love is supposed to hurt. Like Ale, when you've witnessed violence between your parents and that violence is also directed at you, you likely grow up believing that it's normal and you become desensitized to violence. You may also grow up using fighting as a coping strategy to survive (thinking you're resolving) conflict, because that's what you learned from what you saw.

From the polyvagal perspective I described in chapter 3, your neurons begin to adjust and expect violence and betrayal as the norm—so much so that loving relationships are what make you fearful and suspicious and activate your threat response, being seen by your nervous system as the true violation.[13]

The next chapter will help you explore how complex posttraumatic stress impacts your inner world. We'll journey together to learn more about your Self and your own inner parts from an IFS perspective. You'll start to see yourself and all your parts, all having good intentions for you, so you can begin shifting the shame you carry to self-compassion, curiosity, and love. And that's sincerely my wish for you.

CHAPTER 5

Complex Posttraumatic Stress in Our Inner World

How often do you feel alone in the world? Try and answer this truthfully for yourself. Because even when many of us share similar experiences, living with trauma can feel isolating and stigmatizing. Maya Angelou once said, "There's no greater agony than bearing an untold story inside you." It's really scary to disclose to your friends and family that you're hurting, are feeling depressed, or need help. Talking about our feelings to others and risking vulnerability is hard for us. And coming from ancestral lineages with historical trauma, vulnerability is even more of a struggle. But your grief deserves your witness and compassion. To look inward and really witness your feelings may mean remembering things you wanted to forget.

You can no longer turn away from what *is* and *was*, wishing it away for what it should be. Wanting to avoid your painful memories is a way of coping. Just like exiling your vulnerability. Your attempts at survival will differ from those of others struggling with traumatic stress. This is because your inner world, your access to help, and your support systems are unique.

How Complex PTSD Shows Up

Dr. Gabor Maté described trauma to be "not just what happened to you, but what happened inside you in response to what happened to you."[14] So, what happened inside you after what happened to you? What continues to happen inside you when you're trying to keep yourself together for the eyes of others, but are crying inside to be witnessed and understood?

Your pain likely shows up in the language you use talking with others. Like when you often ask someone, "You know?" or "You know what I mean, right?" You're unconsciously asking, "Do you get me?" and "Are you seeing me?" Because we all want to be seen and "gotten." Especially when parts of us have been shunned from the world and our identities rejected. Your pain shows up in all the ways you cope: through perfectionism, self-harm, addiction, restlessness, distraction, narcissism, avoiding people, over- or underindulging in things, disordered eating, overspending, over-studying, and many more ways you're trying to survive what you feel inside.

Even the American Psychological Association recognizes the serious-ness of this situation for Black, Indigenous, and People of Color, stating that "intersectional oppression such as racial, gender, sexual orientation, and xenophobic microaggressions contribute to the cumulative effects of racial trauma."[15] Both complex posttraumatic stress disorder (CPTSD) and posttraumatic stress disorder (PTSD) are born out of situations where you feel powerless in the face of threat and don't receive support. Let me briefly explain to you the difference between PTSD and CPTSD so that you can understand the distinction.

PTSD, also called chronic trauma,[16] relates to sensory flashbacks (or intrusive memories) from a past traumatic experience or series of painful incidents that randomly pop up in your mind in forms such as images, smells, tastes, bodily sensations, and nightmares. These sensory flashbacks activate your threat response.

CPTSD is the result of ongoing exposure to toxic stress. It's often passed down through attachment trauma and legacy burdens. It's the trauma response stemming from relational trauma (like betrayal, xenopho-bic microaggressions, or abuse in any relationship that has you feeling con-tinuously unsafe) or ongoing developmental trauma in childhood that creates attachment wounding (abuse, witnessing violence in the home, abandonment, emotional neglect, sexual abuse). With CPTSD, your threat response (fight, flight, freeze, shutdown) is activated by emotional triggers that remind you of your past painful memories—your terror of violence or punishment, your worry of rejection, your fear of loss. And like I said in this book's introduction, you can also experience intrusive thoughts and memories of times when you were discriminated against, called racial slurs or other oppressive slurs, or abused in any way.

With CPTSD, words people say, things people do, and certain behaviors of others can activate the threat response in your body. Sometimes a phrase that has ties to the past can be an emotional trigger. For instance, racial slurs can elicit emotional triggers and activate your threat response. Or your heart might race when you see a police officer, ICE agent, or anyone who has harmed you or people in your community. Or your body might tense up when you see a Confederate flag hanging. Or someone's pain might bring up memories of your own pain, helplessness, vulnerability, shame, rage, grief, and loss. The list goes on. Sensory flashbacks (like smells, images, sounds, touch, places) can also occur that remind you of past trauma, but, with CPTSD, your threat response is largely evoked by your emotional pain from relational wounding, legacy burdens, and the impact of racism and oppression.

Before I go on, let's take a breath. If you're open, go within and scan your body for any tension. If you notice any pressure or tension, what does it need from you right now? Just notice how you're feeling and breathe into the spaces that feel tense or have discomfort. You don't need to change anything about it. Just notice. And if it feels sincere, extend some care to what you're feeling. When you're ready, continue on...

Let's talk about flashbacks for a moment. If you're having flashbacks, please know that your flashbacks are real and valid. They are also your brain's way of trying to heal itself by showing the unread and unprocessed files that need opening and a place to go. Like stacks of files on a desk that need to be sorted and filed away in their proper place. Using the lens of internal family systems, flashbacks are parts of you stuck in past painful memories, needing witness, retrieval, and healing.

When you have traumatic experiences, your amygdala (the emotional center of the brain) sears your memories of the trauma (e.g., the person who hurt you, place, body sensation) with emotional energy but disregards full narratives. Your brain sends these fragmented memories to consciousness with the hopes that they will be integrated with a full narrative of what happened, sealed, and stored away with closure. Your fear and avoidance to face and process these traumas can have you fluctuating between your actively avoiding these memories and your brain's response to push you to process them through intrusive memories. Your flashbacks have energetic charge to them. They want attention and processing. They want a full narrative of what happened to you—because without it, you will consistently be in a threat response whenever you encounter a similar interaction that isn't necessarily dangerous. Your brain will continue to think you're reliving past trauma because it has no sense of time, only the energy of the past that it's trying to make sense of to keep you safe. Your flashbacks represent an area where your body and brain seek healing. They are truly your self-healing system at work toward resolution.[17]

Intrusive memories can happen in your dreams, show up in daytime thoughts, or occur any time you feel fear because they're linking back to your trauma. Sometimes they are what drives your decisions without you even knowing. They come from the body and brain's instinctual evolutionary design to be prepared if a sudden tragedy were to strike. Unconsciously, intrusive memories have you waiting for the other shoe to drop, holding your breath or breathing shallow because trauma has taught you bad things will happen when you let your guard down.

Your intrusive memories are burdens. They are burdens carried by parts of you that took them on after trauma. Now you might be wondering what I've meant when I've made reference to "parts of you." Let's learn about these parts using the lens of internal family systems.

A "Family" of Parts in Our Brains and Bodies: The Internal Family Systems Perspective

Internal family systems (IFS) therapy is a therapeutic healing practice—and way to see the world—that seeks to humanize our pain, instead of pathologizing it. It teaches that your mind is naturally multiple (as some

Indigenous peoples have long believed), with various "parts" existing and working together to help you navigate and respond to the world. This means we aren't ever really one thing. For example, I am playful, cranky, easily distracted, ambitious, angry, sad, hopeful, hopeless, and a world of contradictions because I'm so many things based on what parts of me are activated, and the burdens these parts carry. You have within you an entire inner constellation of parts that are like an orchestra to a symphony. And your core Self is the conductor.[18]

We are all born with a Self and parts. *You* were born with a Self and parts. Coming from ancestral lineages of trauma, while being born into a system that perpetuates racism against you from birth, and inheriting cultural and familial legacy burdens means that your parts already start to take on burdens from birth. And as you grow, the decisions you make are influenced by these burdens.

Let's use people pleasing as an example. Living as a Black, Indigenous, and Person of Color, you may have developed some parts that caretake and people please to keep you safe or artificially connected to others. Or you might be aware of a part of you that carries rage because of all you've been through and, when activated, might scream at others or implode. You might also be aware of a part that comes in to shut you down when you're feeling your rage.

Like your family members in the outside world, some of these parts get along and some don't. But the most important thing to know about these parts of you is that they always have the best intentions for you in mind and do what they do to protect you and keep you from getting hurt again— no matter how destructive they seem to you or the outside world. They help you cope with the only survival strategies they know. These parts are burdened with extreme roles because of what's been done to you and, if given a chance, would rather do something else—not navigate racism and other relational trauma. It's important to know that your parts aren't their burdens or their survival strategies. Parts adopt coping strategies based on what helps them best deal with their environments and the people around them, or mirror what they've seen others do. How do *your* parts cope? Let's get a sense of what your coping looks like with curiosity. Just get to know the strategies in place that serve to protect you, however unhealthy they appear to the outside (and inside) world.

REFLECTION PRACTICE:
How Your Parts Cope

Step 1: Open your heart to you for a moment. Acknowledge your Self, your protector parts (proactive and reactive parts), and the vulnerable parts of you that are exiled. What sense do you get? Feel free to write down what stands out to you, or just witness.

Step 2: Your coping strategies can reveal how parts of yourself are burdened. In chapter 2, I briefly introduced a list of survival strategies. If you were able to journal about it, or reflect on it, I invite you to review that list (and add to it if needed). It identifies the coping strategies you use when you're feeling activated and/or shut down.

Step 3: Next to each strategy on the list, write if you think it's a proactive strategy to avoid pain, or a reactive strategy to numb out pain.

Step 4: Then ask, who within you uses these strategies? Consider humanizing the part using these strategies to protect you if that feels right. If this part were a person, what role would they be playing in your life? Would they be the one always telling you to look on the bright side or dismiss your pain with toxic positivity? Would they be the one often reminding you of all the dangers in the world? Would they be the one telling you to be quiet to avoid punishment? Would they be the one blaming you for everything?

Step 5: When you're done, I just want you to notice how you're feeling toward these parts of you. Be curious about what comes up, write it down in your journal if you want, and ask yourself what needs to happen within for you to feel more compassion toward them (if you don't already). They work really hard to keep you safe, sometimes in extreme, hurtful ways, but always with the intention to help you.

Your Core Self

Just as you're born with parts, you're also born with a Self. Your Self is your inner wisdom. It's what some folks call your essence or higher Self. It's you at your core. What feels so hopeful about the Self is that it can never be traumatized. Your Self, no matter what happens to you, is always preserved. That's why you can never be broken. You can never be damaged. You can certainly be hurting, but even with your hurt, *you will always be intact and whole*. Read that last part again. And your Self can bring healing to all your parts by witnessing and helping them release their burdens. Your Self embodies eight "Cs." They are:

- Compassion

- Creativity

- Courage

- Confidence

- Connectedness

- Clarity

- Calmness

- Curiosity

When you are leading from Self, you are embodying these qualities. But let's be real—you will not always be Self-led. We alternate between Self and parts often. The goal is for your Self to be the spokesperson for your parts—like a president speaking on behalf of their nation. You speak *for* your parts, rather than *from* them, when you can. This is why "Choice" can be considered an unofficial ninth quality of Self, because speaking *for* what you're feeling rather than *from* what you're feeling can help you connect with your power and be more intentional with your response. Frank Anderson has shared that "Self is a resource for your parts, and your parts are also a resource for your Self."[19]

Your Parts

Let's go a little deeper into parts. Remember that all your parts have good intentions, and that parts serve different roles. We can break parts down into two general categories: protector parts and exiled parts.

YOUR PROTECTOR PARTS

Protection can come in many forms, but there are two main types of parts that take on protective roles within you. Let's look at these now.

The firefighter. These are the parts of you inside that behave like fire-fighters in a fire. They jump in, break glass if they need to, and do whatever needs to be done to extinguish the fire. They are your reactive parts that carry the burden of distracting you from connecting to the vulnerable parts of you that are cast away. These firefighter parts are sometimes the ones that cast away these vulnerable parts (when the world isn't getting first dibs on exiling them). Their job is to shut down and numb any traumatic memories or feelings of pain and vulnerability by any means necessary. Some common survival strategies of firefighter parts are binge eating, drinking to cope, dissociation, self-harm, attempting suicide, fighting, and overspending.[20]

The manager. And then there are parts that take on a more managerial role. These are the parts of you inside that behave like bosses. They are more proactive and act preemptively, carrying the burden of attempting to control others and the environment (and your other parts) so that you're not hurt again. Your manager parts can be controlling, critical of you and others (hello, inner critic), suspicious, pessimistic, overly analytical, perfectionistic, intellectualizing, and overthinking.

Burdened manager and firefighter parts live in the brain and express themselves through a dysregulated nervous system.[21] This means that when your protector parts are activated, you will experience a threat response in your body and go into a state of fight, flight, freeze, or shutdown. Navigating racism and oppression sends your protective parts—and thus your body's threat response—into overdrive. These protector parts believe they are responsible for protecting your Self, not only from the danger of the outside world, but also from what they see as the inner dangers of vulnerability and from the parts of you that hold your most painful memories: the exiled parts.

YOUR EXILED PARTS

These are the vulnerable parts of you that are exiled from your awareness. They carry your most painful wounding (which is why your protector parts repress them or feel the added responsibility to protect them). For instance, when a firefighter part is raging toward others, it's defending a vulnerable part of you holding a deep wound of sadness. Your exiled parts are often young and frozen in time after experiencing trauma. They are your inner children. When your exiled parts are present in your body, you might find yourself feeling raw, sensitive, and with your emotions on the surface, or experiencing flashbacks and intrusive memories. Your exiled parts want their story to be witnessed and don't want to be forgotten. They need your Self-love, curiosity, and compassion—like all of your inner system.

Wow! What a journey so far. If you'd like, take a deep breath and stretch before we begin our reflection practice. When you're ready, take a moment and reflect on your inside world.

What does your inner world look like? It can be incredibly powerful to visualize it and externalize your internal system to see how you'd represent your parts. Gaining a sense of how your inner world is represented within can help you develop more of a connection with all the parts of you and open your heart toward them. For our next practice, I invite you to gather some markers, crayons, pencils, pens, paint, magazines—whatever art supplies you feel compelled to use.

REFLECTION PRACTICE:
Picture Your Inner World

I invite you to engage your creativity (a quality of Self) to create pictures of your inner world. Create some kind of visual image of your Self, and what your protector parts and exiled parts look like. You can draw, paint, color, or cut out pictures from a magazine to create an illustration or a collage. You can also choose to use a scrapbook for this activity. No art skills needed here. Just your willingness to be creative and go inside yourself to get acquainted with your inner world.

As you do, consider where your parts are in proximity to each other on the page. Which parts help each other and which parts are at odds, working against each other? Take your time with this exercise. Don't be afraid to be creative and go all out if you want to. It's such a gift to be able to see what you look like on the inside.

Know that you can add to this illustration, or series of images, any time a new part presents itself to you. Remember that your protector parts carry burdens and take on extreme roles—but they aren't their burdens. Your Self can help them unburden slowly and safely, in time, when it feels right. Our parts help us cope. Our Self helps us heal. What might it look like for your parts to put down all the burdens they're carrying? How does your Self help them do this? Try drawing it.

To Wrap It All Up...

We all want our pain to be witnessed. Deep down, our exiled parts wish to tell our story and our protector parts really work hard to protect us from being harmed again. We live much of our lives trying to feel or not feel, and our parts use strategies to help this agenda—always with good intentions, even when it doesn't land that way. Our flashbacks and intrusive memories serve as communication to us of the hurt we're holding and comes from our innate longing and power to heal ourselves.

Next we'll begin the second empowerment step, where you'll be practicing how to mend shame and shaming beliefs with self-compassion. Just so you know, your parts carrying shame can be exiled parts and can also be a protector part (like your inner critic). So I encourage you to be curious when we explore shame further. Ask yourself, *Are these my shaming parts (protector)? Or my shamed parts (exiled)?*

Take care of yourself, love. Take a break. Drink some water. Use the bathroom. Listen to your body and offer yourself some care right now. See you in chapter 6 when you're ready.

Second Empowerment Step: Mend Shame and Shaming Beliefs with Self-Compassion

Shame creates disconnection in relationships and completely interferes with your own self-love. You might've begun feeling shame early in your life when someone took advantage of your vulnerability. Brené Brown, a leading researcher of shame and vulnerability, defined shame as a painful feeling or experience of believing we're flawed and unworthy of love and belonging.[22] It's a judgment of your character, who you are as a whole, and a painful burden often carried by your vulnerable inner child(ren). Shame says, "I'm bad" or "Something is wrong with me." And the more vulnerable you feel with little (or no) support, the stronger your shame becomes. Shame attempts to tell you that you're unlovable. And we all want to be loved.

What are your earliest memories with shame? How old were you when you began feeling ashamed of yourself? Who shamed you? Take a moment to notice any scenes, messages, or voices that show themselves to you. Feel free to write them down in your journal.

I feel like there are many instances when you learn and internalize shame: from the toxic societal systems you grow up in to the harm you might face if you're a survivor of child abuse and neglect. *Cultural legacy burdens, family legacy burdens, and personal burdens are fed by shame.* This is true for all the isms, as you're shamed for being who you are within racist and oppressive systems.

As you continue to grow in societal systems that were oppressive toward you, different parts may emerge in you that try to help you cope and survive in them, as we touched on in the last chapter. When it comes to shame, you may have developed a critical part of you that has replaced those who've shamed and criticized you. This shaming part (oftentimes taking the form of an inner critic) might have taken on the burden of shaming you to protect you somehow.

Perhaps by shaming you, your inner critic feels like it can keep you focused and aiming toward higher goals. Or perhaps the burden it carries is to keep you small so you don't speak up and risk further harm by authority or dominant groups. My inner critic sometimes tries to keep me feeling small. Coping in this way helps me to avoid conflict. If I feel small and ashamed, there's less possibility for me to speak up and ruffle some feathers. I'll feel less inclined to rock the boat, and therefore will stay in my lane. If I do that, I'll have significantly less conflict with the outside world— though my inner world will be raging and full of conflicts as I walk through life feeling invisible.

What about you? I'm curious about how cultural legacy burdens, legacy burdens inherited from family intergenerationally, and personal burdens from trauma you've experienced have impacted your inner world.

Some Roles of Your Protector Parts

What are some of the *roles* of your protector parts, what burdens are they carrying, and what vulnerable exiled part of you are they protecting? Consider how these roles have also been passed down intergenerationally as legacy burdens. Many of these roles can be legacy burdens inherited from behavioral patterns in a family. Here's a list of some common ones that might resonate with you:

> **The inner critic/inner judge:** This part can take on the role of shaming you in an attempt to motivate you to succeed or judge others so that you feel better than them and, therefore, good enough. Sometimes your inner shamer might shame other parts because that's what it learned to do to keep you meeting society's expectations of you—to avoid the burden of rejection and being othered.

The inner child(ren): This exiled part can carry the pain of being abused, neglected, othered, abandoned, and so on, and is typically what our protector parts protect. However, our protector parts can also be young, and sometimes they carry the burden of protecting the even younger parts of us.

The people pleaser: This part can carry the burden of pleasing others (to your own detriment) for fear of hurting their feelings, avoiding conflict, being rejected, experiencing loss, or making people mad at you.

The strong one: This part can take on the role of having to be strong, tolerate pain, and not express your needs because of fear they'll be seen as complaints. It believes it needs to adopt this role to avoid being seen as weak if you feel vulnerable. You might've often heard the message "Be strong, don't cry" and have internalized the belief that visibly showing emotions isn't welcomed. This part might tell you to push through the pain, push through the grief, push through the exhaustion. It might demand you "pull yourself up by your bootstraps!" Like Luisa Madrigal in Disney's movie *Encanto*, the part of you burdened with being strong can feel the pressure of keeping it together and deep down really wants relief to embrace vulnerability.

The shutdown one: This part can take on the duty to dissociate, numb out, and shut down temporarily or more long term when you're feeling fear, discomfort, anger, and vulnerability. This part can come in to help save you from hurtful experiences in the moment. Sometimes we don't even know we're dissociating because it can be an unconscious, reflexive response to feeling pain that an exiled part is carrying.

The bypasser: This part can dismiss your pain from the past (and that of others) and cover it up with joy to prevent staying hurt. This part can use toxic positivity to try to help you see things as only good to prevent hopelessness. Sometimes this part tries to get you to override your grief and pain rather than to witness and be with the fullness of it. It might persuade you to move on and not look back.

The self-sacrificing one: This part can carry the burden of responsibility for others. It might demand that you abandon your needs to put the needs of others before yours. This may be for approval, pleasing others, avoiding discomfort owning your feelings and needs, or fear of conflict. This part might also often assume the role of caretaker of others.

The drill sergeant: This part can adopt the role of being rigid, unforgiving, stoic, demanding, and controlling to get others to obey commands, to protect exiled parts that are feeling helpless and powerless, or to keep things in order, predictable, and familiar.

The perfectionist: This part can carry the burden of perfectionism to avoid rejection or punishment, encourage belonging, feel worthy and lovable, and avoid feeling flawed.

The overthinker/overanalyzer: This part might believe it needs to obsessively think things through to avoid making mistakes, being rejected, or being shamed, and to remain feeling in control. This part might also want to get it right and make things predictable to feel safer.

The self-loather: This part can have you hating yourself to protect you from the hate and rejection of others. It may anticipate the continued hate and rejection of others and want to "beat them to the punch" so that others' disapproval of you hurts less than your own.

The chameleon/shape-shifter: Similar to people pleasing, this part can carry the burden of camouflaging, folding, and shrinking, or fawning (being inauthentic) to reduce threat and punishment.

The intellectual: This part can urge you to stay in your head to avoid closeness, vulnerability, and emotions. It can feel safer to stay in your head than open your heart to feeling. This part attempts to protect you from being hurt and wants to help you feel worthy and valuable, by knowing all the answers or being able to rationalize things away. Having all the answers can help keep life more predictable and make more people see your value, and thus love and accept you. It wants you to belong, like many of your protector parts.

The fatigued one: Exhaustion and chronic fatigue can be a sign of an overworked protector part, sometimes causing pain and illness (or exacerbating pain and illness that was already there) as a way of communicating to you to slow down if you're doing too much. Sometimes this part may use chronic fatigue to prevent you from taking on more tasks if it doesn't trust you to slow down.

The distractor: This part can take on the role of frequently distracting you from important tasks. It may help you procrastinate or detach from discomfort for long periods of time. Its mission might be to help you avoid your feelings and interfere with your success or joy because it's afraid of you failing or succeeding.

The code-switcher: This part can carry the burden of "tone policing" you so that you're received well in predominantly White spaces. It may believe you need to hide your accent and speak with an expansive vocabulary. Its strategy is to have you assimilate to be accepted, seen as valuable, and afforded the same opportunities as White bodies within racist systems.

The pessimist: This part's role can interfere with your hope and joy to avoid disappointment. It may not want you to feel optimism, because it holds anticipatory loss and is afraid. If you're constantly expecting disappointment, you're not as surprised when it happens and it "doesn't hurt as much."

Although I've named these roles, they're simply to give you a sense of what some roles might be. They aren't the names or identities of your parts. Your parts aren't their roles or the burdens they carry. That said, are there any other roles of your protector parts you're aware of that aren't on this list? Think about what burden they might carry and why. Now, if you're open to it, I invite you to get to know some of your protector parts more. Let's start with your inner critic, if that feels right. If your inner critic carries the burden of shame, you're likely finding yourself in a tussle with a voice that puts you down and makes it hard to love and accept yourself. Then I'll invite you to practice getting to know your inner child(ren) using the reflection practices ahead. You'll begin to explore past experiences of little you with more compassion—the same compassion you might've wished you received from your family (and the world) during these hurtful moments.

Getting to Know Your Burden of Shame

The goal is to get to know your inner world of parts better. The more you can befriend and mend your relationship with your protective and vulnerable parts, the more connected you will feel to them and they will feel to you. And the more you will begin to deeply understand and rebuild trust in yourself and have confidence in your intuition.

Let's start with some questions for your inner critic (or inner shamer). These questions are what IFS therapists typically ask when guiding their clients inside their inner world to spend time with their parts. Ask your inner critic these questions, one by one, and write down their answers in your journal:

- How long have you been around?

- Whose voice do you represent?

- What are you trying to protect me from?

- How are you trying to help me?

- How do you communicate to me through my body?

- What are you afraid would happen if you didn't criticize or shame me? Where else in my life has that happened?

- How did shaming me become so important for you to do?

- How can you show love and concern differently?

- What would you rather be doing than carrying this burden of shaming me?

- How can we work together to release these burdens you're carrying so that you can be who you're truly meant to be?

What was that like for you? Know that whatever comes up for you is welcome. You might find you're a ball of emotions. Or you might find that you're calm. Whatever you find is a gift of information to learn more about yourself.

If you'd like, after asking your inner critic these questions, you're welcome to choose other protector parts to get to know. The more the merrier. Ask them these questions and any others that intuitively come up for you (you can use the list above or the inner world illustration you completed in chapter 5 as a reference). Be curious and extend that curiosity to the parts that come up for you.

REFLECTION PRACTICE:
Witnessing the Scenes of Your Life

Consider what you learned hearing the answers to these questions, and when you're ready, let's take it a step further. Let's walk a trail of memories with a part calling for your attention. In IFS therapy, there's a sacred process of fully seeing the burdens of our parts, called *witnessing*. When you witness all of the pain your vulnerable parts have been holding for a long time, it paves the way for them to release the burdens they're carrying. However, with complex posttraumatic stress and with cultural legacy burdens, unburdening happens in layers—because you are still living in a racist and oppressive system.

Step 1: I invite you to choose a part (or parts) to walk through a trail of scenes in your life with, where there's unwitnessed pain. You might want to choose from the parts that carry legacy and personal burdens that I listed earlier in this chapter. You can start with your earliest childhood memory, or a scene that comes up for you organically from your childhood or adolescence. Just walk this path toward this memory for a moment. Notice what you see, who's there, and what's happening in this scene. What do you want to believe about yourself as you see yourself there?

Step 2: See if you're able to connect with a younger version of yourself. When that happens, can you offer compassion to this younger you? What kind of care is it needing from you? Listen to all that your younger you shares with you. Let it know you're there and that your heart is open toward it, if that feels sincere. Befriend it. Be with it the way you needed someone to be there for you.

Step 3: What are the words younger you most needed to hear in that memory? If it feels sincere, say these words to them. Let little you of the past know that the you of today sees what they went through and all they did so that you could be here today.

Step 4: If it seems possible, you might even ask this younger version of you if you can get them from this past scene and take them somewhere safe they'd rather be. In IFS therapy, we call this process of an unburdening a *retrieval*. What's a place of safety and joy for this younger you? Ask the you of today the same question.

If your younger you is not able to identify a safe place, they can imagine one. Take them there if they want. If not, just continue to spend time witnessing the scenes they wish to share with you.

Step 5: Continue deepening your relationship with this younger you using your Self energy (the core energy of your Self). The more you take time to witness, the more trust you gain. If it feels right, offer gratitude to the younger version of you for doing all they did with what little they knew to keep you safe back then.

Let's take a pause for a moment. Breathe if that's what you need. Stretch. Give yourself a compassionate touch. Maybe you might want to offer yourself an embrace, using the practice you learned in chapter 3: *abrazo mariposa* (the butterfly hug). Inhale. Slowly exhale. You've done some powerful sacred work just now.

When you're ready, get your journal or a piece of paper and pen (or use your computer). You're going to write a letter to your inner child, or younger version of yourself. Our inner children are usually the parts we exile because they can remind us of all the pain and helplessness we felt as kids. It can be really difficult to feel tenderness toward any parts of you that carry any semblance of vulnerability. And yet, the deep healing work lies here with your protector parts in extreme roles trying to protect your more vulnerable, exiled parts. Would you be open to connecting more with your young parts? With your permission, let's move closer to little you. You can start by writing them a letter.

WRITING PRACTICE:
Letter to Your Inner Child

Your inner child has likely been exiled from your awareness for a long time. The most vulnerable parts of us tend to be young. They are also the parts of us that have been around forever. When you consider how long parts of you have been around, and you get a sense they're super old, know that this really means these parts are young. Many times, they are frozen in time and stuck in the past, waiting to be witnessed and liberated.

Here's a sample of my letter to my inner child. If my words resonate with yours, please feel free to tell yourself these words and more. Give yourself these words with an open heart, channeling your compassion, courage, and other "C" qualities of your Self. Remember, your Self brings healing to your inner child (and all your parts) as you continue to witness their story and love them through it.

Dear little me, thank you. I couldn't have made it without you. You went through pain no one should ever go through. I'm sorry it happened. You deserved so much more. You deserved safety, love, and your full childhood. I don't know how you did it, but I'm grateful you did. Thank you for surviving all you went through, and doing all you did, so I could be here today. You worked so hard as a kid to keep us safe and that was so unfair. It isn't always easy to face you, but I'm learning. I want to repay you and show you what it's like to feel safety again. I want to give you all you deserve. I'm doing what I can and can take care of us now. Rest, little me. I'll take it from here...

Take the time to write your inner child(ren) a heartfelt letter. Little you has worked so hard to keep you safe for a really long time. And I want you to know, everything you did (or didn't do) when you were little to keep yourself safe was the right thing to do. Little you needs your Self to witness all they've been holding. They need your tenderness and open heart. They need you to be a champion for them now. I'm so glad they have you. Tell your little you that they are worth your time.

This next practice offers another way to honor your inner child.

SPIRITUAL PRACTICE:
Make an Inner Child Altar

Just as you may have altars to honor your ancestors, you can also consider creating an altar to honor your little you. To stay connected to them and give them the care they may not have gotten in the ways they needed. You can begin to give to them what you needed, starting with acknowledgment.

Your altar can be as creative or as simple as you want it to be. You can frame a picture of the little you you'd like to connect with more, or who still carries pain. Put this picture of them in a place you can see. If you don't have a picture, you can draw yourself, get a toy figurine, or find something that represents you at that age. You can also put the letter you wrote to them on this altar. Or write a new one to leave on the altar.

Make it a daily practice to look at their picture and say kind words. Consider making it a morning and evening ritual. Maybe even light a candle for them. On your birthday, let them know you celebrate them too. This can help facilitate closeness with the younger you that has been exiled.

I just want to pause right here and extend the invitation for you to stretch and walk around where you are for a moment. Maybe rest your eyes for a few seconds. Drink some water. When you're ready, let's do one more inner child exercise together.

JOURNALING PRACTICE:
Internalized Childhood Messages

Step 1: If you have access to baby pictures or photos of younger versions of yourself, choose one and tape it to the center of a page in your journal or a separate piece of paper. If you don't have any pictures of yourself, you can draw yourself or write your name and age in the center of the paper and draw a circle around it.

Step 2: Around your childhood photo (or representation of it), jot down all the negative messaging told to you by your caregivers, teachers, society, family members, and friends when you were growing up. Encircling the photo (not on the photo), write all the hurtful words you heard at that age to describe you—and who said them if you remember.

Step 3: On a separate piece of paper, write the messages you wished you heard. Give these new messages to yourself. Write them down, and if it feels right, leave the paper by your altar or by a mirror that you use daily. Let these be your new affirmations. You might certainly struggle with self-esteem issues, but what else is true? Could you still be enough?

To Wrap It All Up...

Offering yourself compassion can be one of the hardest things to do and also the most necessary. You've been taught to treat yourself like a burden. And as a Black, Indigenous, and Person of Color, an important part of your healing journey is to shift the burden of shame you carry to a place of curiosity and compassion. Curiosity helps you stay open and willing to understand your story more. It helps create empathy, which can inform compassion. Shame doesn't leave room for empathy or compassion. Ironically, the more you try to understand your shame's story, the more you'll find that deep down, shame feels vulnerable. And that your inner critic can be so vile at times, because they live in fear.

The beautiful truth of all this is that you have the ability to hold your parts, no matter what. You have the ability to show up for yourself, in all the ways you needed as a child or an adolescent. And you have the capacity to heal yourself. *You* are the source. So, even in your darkest hour, where life seems to be falling apart and you feel like you can't hold on any longer, know that even in the face of danger, it's possible to hold your parts.[23] When you witness the little you and other parts of you, you are never alone.

I'm sending your protector parts and the parts within you that have been exiled some love. You've done such profound work, and rest is a necessary part of your healing. This work happens in layers over time. Take a minute to rest your mind, body, and spirit before heading on to part III. We'll be exploring attachment wounding with legacy burdens passed down through intergenerational trauma, and we'll reconnect with the legacy resources of our ancestors. We inherited not just their pain, but also their wisdom and strength. See you there.

We Carry the Pain and Resources of Our Ancestors

Your pain is not all of you. And you are not your pain. There's so much more to your life than that. I know that might be hard to believe when a big chunk of your life has been filled with trying to survive and you feel like pain and suffering are all you know. I remember reading this quote by Oprah in her most recent book with Dr. Bruce Perry that left an imprint in my heart. She was vulnerably sharing her experience preparing for her mother's transition and said, "We don't have to keep the pain alive to keep the truth alive."[24] Oof. This was such a powerful message. How many of us carry pain because we fear that releasing it means we also surrender our story? Or fear that releasing pain means the people who hurt us get away with it?

If you can relate to that, is this also true for the legacy burdens you carry for your family and ancestors? Sometimes we hold on to their legacy burdens because we're afraid of losing connection to our family or ancestors, or feel like we're dishonoring or betraying them if we feel less pain. Sometimes we might hold on to legacy burdens because we fear losing our identities.[25]

But most times, living in a structurally racist and oppressive system can have you holding on tightly to both cultural and family legacy burdens because these burdens remind you of what is needed from you to survive. You unconsciously hold these burdens because they can help you cope temporarily. For instance, if you're carrying a cultural legacy burden of racism that has contributed to legacy burdens in your family, one belief might be that your racialized identity is intimidating to White folks. If so, you might be conditioned to tone down some of who you are (like colorful aspects of your personality, your fire and passion, your emphatic voice, your hair and clothing) to belong. We are trained to police our tone of voice. We do this to make White people comfortable, to avoid being seen as threatening, and maybe to take up less space.

If you carry a cultural legacy burden of racism that translates to assimilating to Whiteness, you might code-switch and hide your accent in predominantly White spaces (like work environments). You may do this to mitigate being othered and gain some acceptance—because to be discriminated against and feel othered or devalued in the workplace can interfere with your being promoted, keeping your job, or having your skills seen. And we all have skills. But in a racist system, we all don't have the same opportunities.

It makes sense to me that sometimes carrying legacy burdens as you continue journeying through life with a racialized identity (and other marginalized identities) can feel like an armor of protection. Similar to if you were living with a partner who was abusive toward you. The survival tools that keep you safe in a dangerous relationship or environment can feel too risky to release when you're still there. But what if I told you that it's possible to slowly release these burdens and instead summon the resources from your legacy? That you don't have to surrender your truth (or that of your ancestors) if you begin releasing some of the pain you carry? That releasing legacy burdens can actually give you a fuller sense of your identity and strengthen your connection with your ancestors? Because you cannot just live in the pain of your story and the story of your lineage. You must first deeply understand and witness all of the pain, which creates space in your heart for other feelings and for more access to your inner wisdom. Compassion lives in that place in your heart between witnessing your pain and acknowledging that your reactions to these struggles have all come from a place of survival and trying to help yourself the only ways you know how.

And it feels important to name here, that releasing legacy burdens can also feel like a privilege. Not everyone, especially those in present danger, can afford or have the power to release burdens that might help keep them alive. I'm thinking of many Communities of Color, LGBTQIA2S+, and neurodivergent folks with various abilities, all marginalized and holding burdens that feel hard to put down when you're anticipating the next time you'll need to pick them up again. The more you can open your heart up to your own coping tools and reasons why you do what you do, the more empathy and compassion you can offer to others with similar pain as yours.

As we make space to witness the pain you carry and that you inherited from your ancestry, let's also begin making room for the resources you've inherited from your ancestors. We'll talk more about intergenerational trauma, the grief infused in the patterns of abuse and disconnection across generations, and how historical trauma created legacy burdens in your family. Remember that the wounding you have seen and learned from your family has been taught to them by the system. They, too, have been impacted. And like many of us, they continue to pass down harmful behaviors and burdens unintentionally. But if we know better, we have a greater chance to do better and journey with more awareness toward our liberation. One day at a time. One generation at a time. Like Aiyana and her daughters...

CHAPTER 7

Aiyana, Dakota, and Malia's Story (she/her)

Aiyana is a forty-four-year-old Native American cisgender woman living in Tohatchi, New Mexico, just outside of Gallup on the Navajo Nation reservation. Aiyana has two adult cisgender daughters, Dakota, who is twenty-seven, and Malia, who is twenty-two. Aiyana works in Gallup as a hotel clerk and lives with her daughters' father, Paco, despite a strained relationship, to try to stay afloat financially. Aiyana and Paco's relationship has been volatile many times in the past, with frequent verbal and emotional abuse, and at times, physical violence.

Aiyana had a distant relationship with her parents, who struggled with health issues and lived in a poorly maintained nursing home. Her parents had both been neglectful to Aiyana in her childhood, and essentially disowned her when she became pregnant with Dakota at seventeen years old. Due to this separation from her immediate family, Aiyana lost a lot of connection to her heritage, her grandparents, and her wider community that left her without support.

Aiyana also described a sense of scarcity. She constantly felt there was never enough money for food, clothing, or hobbies all her life. There was also never enough love for Aiyana, and she'd often tell herself she was unlovable and undeserving. Aiyana's struggle with this sense of scarcity (what some call a "scarcity mindset") grew from being marginalized and witnessing violence in her home and not having the love she needed in childhood. There was never enough; therefore, she felt she was never

enough. Scarcity, when you grow up with minimal means financially, emotionally, and spiritually, can make life feel incomplete. Both supremacy
culture and capitalism can create the legacy burden that says, "There isn't
enough for all," sometimes leading us to fight with each other and compete
for opportunities and wealth. We are rarely taught that there can be abundance, including the outflow of love from community.

Aiyana described her own childhood as scary and lonely. She remem-
bered her parents' deep depression, substance use, and anxiety throughout
those years. Aiyana would often try to gain the approval of her parents and
community, until she just gave up and looked for love elsewhere. That's
when she met Paco.

Aiyana now has a growing relationship with her two daughters after
doing several years of therapy and trying hard to repair their relationship.
Aiyana shared that one of the hardest times in her life was as a very young
mom raising Dakota. Aiyana admits that Dakota grew up witnessing her
and Paco's fights and sometimes got between them during the altercations
or when something was being thrown. As a young adult, Dakota was
abusive in her relationships.

Malia didn't feel genuine love in her family and didn't really know
what love was. She struggled with loving herself and what that even meant.
She wondered how she could ever love herself when it wasn't really modeled.
Malia's example of love was one that was paired with violence, similar to
Maria Alejandra's in chapter 4. Just like Dakota's and Aiyana's. They were
all taught that love was supposed to hurt, a pattern and belief (legacy
burden) passed down unconsciously throughout the family's generations as
intergenerational trauma.

If this experience is similar to yours and you need to pause for a
moment, I invite you to put your hand over your heart, or take a deep
breath, stretch, hum a tune that you find soothing, or care for yourself in
any other way that feels best for you right now. When you've done that,
let's reflect.

Shared Experience: Intergenerational Trauma

Aiyana and her daughters' experiences depict three generations of wounding on repeat. Like a remix to an original song, the theme is the same except with a different rhythm and melody. This is what intergenerational trauma looks and sounds like. It's trauma passed down throughout the generations. Most of the time, these origins of multigenerational patterns of abuse are based in historical trauma. Aiyana's family lineage carries the pain of genocide and colonization. Her parents used substances to numb the emotional pain and emptiness within.

If you or a loved one is struggling with an addiction, at the crux of your or their actions is an attempt at finding a solution (even if it's superficial) to the core problem: pain and suffering. Using substances to soothe is a coping strategy to suppress deep-rooted trauma. And any time you feel vulnerable, or have intrusive thoughts around any painful experiences (or find yourself reliving them), you may naturally search for an out and numb your feelings with substances and other survival (and self-medicating) strategies. You can look at substance use as a firefighter part trying to be protective of you, even when it's self-sabotaging and comes across as toxic behavior to the outside world. As I mentioned in chapter 2, these symptoms are trailheads to a deeper issue needing your attention and healing.

I'm curious, what did you learn about love from the people who raised you? Like Aiyana and her daughters, you may know what it's like to grow up in an abusive household. You may know that deep fear of seeing your caregivers hitting each other, one hitting the other, or things being thrown around. You may even share Dakota's experience of getting in between your parents and trying to stop them from fighting.

I remember the fear of getting in between my parents when they were arguing, anticipating violence to break out at any moment. And I remember yelling the words "I hate you!" because my little heart held so much anger, disappointment, and fear that I couldn't express because I was too young to have the words and know all that I was feeling. But if you've grown up witnessing abuse between caregivers, these violent experiences impact what you learn about love. Aiyana, Dakota, and Malia learned that love hurt. That love and violence were one and the same. Many kids grow up getting the wires of love and violence crossed when they've witnessed violence in their home, and eventually believe love and betrayal go together. Aiyana witnessed violence in her home growing up, and found herself in a relationship with Paco that was abusive. Their daughters then witnessed violence growing up in the home with Aiyana and Paco, an unfortunate result of intergenerational trauma. Dakota would then become involved in abusive relationships, just like her mother—and surely the many people who came before them.

You may have learned early in life that love was supposed to hurt, and you'll need to unlearn this either before or after you find yourself in abusive relationships in adulthood, or perpetuate that abuse on to others yourself. Love is not synonymous with abuse and violence. To be clear, this doesn't mean that people who've been abusive and explosive toward you don't love you. I don't think it's that simple and that polarized. They might actually care a lot about you. But parts of them have learned to use violence to intimidate and get their needs met and gain your obedience. The child who is hit growing up says, "They hit me because they love me and I need to do better." This same child eventually becomes an adult who partially believes that they deserve violence and punishment for expressing needs or living authentically in their relationships. If *you* were this child who was hit or dismissed, you will learn to dismiss your needs and boundaries just like in childhood. You unconsciously become your own punisher. Does this feel familiar?

It also makes sense why Dakota had difficult relationships. When you grow up in a household with parents who controlled you or betrayed you through abuse or neglect, you're probably going to have a hard time trusting people because adults in your childhood weren't good to you. Not all children will have positive relationships with authority figures if people with more power caused them pain and suffering. You may have an aversion to following rules and rebel against them, or the pendulum may swing to the other extreme and you became resigned.

If this was you, you might have learned to people please, prioritizing other people's feelings and putting them before your own. You might've also learned to shrink yourself to make others comfortable and assimilate to your environment for survival, like the chameleon. And with racial trauma, you might've found yourself in childhood and in adulthood tending to the feelings of White people too, trying to avoid their misplaced anger or disapproval of you. Even when there's a part of you that loathes yourself after you do it. And that caretaking of White people's feelings comes from the cultural legacy burden of racism.

Reflection

I invite you to write in your journal what you learned about love and honoring your needs. As we now know, the love we see or don't see is the love we emulate and seek in the future.

JOURNALING PRACTICE:
What I Learned About Love

Take a moment to answer these questions in your notebook:

- What did I learn about love?

- Did love feel safe to me?

- What messages did I receive about love growing up?

- When, if ever, did I learn to fear love?

- Whom did I go to for love when I was hurting?

I also want to invite you to think about how you have learned to fight, based on how you saw conflict growing up. I'd like to help you get a better sense of what you learned about anger and fighting.

We learn conflict resolution from what we see growing up, and we often emulate it, whether consciously or subconsciously. These patterns of conflict can continue being learned and passed down throughout the generations. If you witnessed violence in your home, you might also try to resolve conflicts through aggression—or you might go to the other extreme and avoid conflict instead. Neither of these extremes help us get our needs met.

REFLECTION PRACTICE:
What I Learned About Conflict

Step 1: I invite you to reflect on how you respond to conflict with friends, family, your children, colleagues, partners, and strangers. If you'd like, write down the patterns you notice, and what activates your threat response right before the conflict. These questions can help guide your reflection:

- How do I avoid conflict? How often do I people please?

- How easy is it for me to set clear boundaries with others?

- How often am I yelling, screaming, or hitting?

- How does my body tell me that I am angry?

- When I am angry, where do I feel it in my body?

Step 2: Now write down how you saw your caregivers and family manage conflict throughout your childhood and adolescence. How are your responses similar? How are they different?

Take note of your reflections, if you choose. Bring them with you (whether you've written them on paper or in your mind) as you move into the next chapter on attachment wounding and grief in historical and intergenerational trauma. People pleasing, avoidance, and caretaking behaviors are coping strategies when you feel threatened by someone or something in your environment. Some of these behaviors were also learned from elders, who adopted these survival strategies from legacy burdens of historical trauma.

Let's talk more about attachment wounding as it moves down the generations, originating from historical and ancestral trauma. And as an aside, it's important to know that the roles you play in your family (whether biological or adopted) growing up, and the ones modeled to you, tend to be the roles you unintentionally take on in your friendships and other relationships. I am looking forward to continuing this work with you. Get some rest and see you in chapter 8.

Attachment Wounding and Grief in Historical and Intergenerational Trauma

Your ancestors were gravely impacted by historical trauma. After enduring hundreds of years of colonization, genocide, enslavement, war, famine, and imperialism, trauma undoubtedly stayed in their bodies and rewired their nervous systems. As you read in chapter 2, changes happen in the way genes communicate after living through ongoing toxic stress. This has happened with your surviving ancestors, and these genetic changes were passed down from generation to generation. Generational injuries are passed down through genetics, attachment wounding, and legacy burdens. This is known as intergenerational trauma. *Historical trauma is the genesis of intergenerational trauma.* In other words, intergenerational trauma is a ramification of historical trauma, transferring years of pain and grief down your lineages.

Resmaa Menakem, an expert on racialized trauma, said, "Racism steals lands. Racism participates in enslavement, colonialism, imperialism, etc."[26] Remember that cultural legacy burdens absorbed from historical trauma—and the "isms" from the larger systems you grew up in—have influenced your family's legacy burdens. And many of these legacy burdens are centuries old and came from a desire to survive, sometimes by any means necessary. It's possible that many of your family's legacy burdens come from the burdens of your ancestors, who tried to survive following the aftermath of a litany of violence—being who they needed to be, doing what they needed to do, hiding what needed to be hidden, and learning how to act in the world if they wanted a chance at life.

Many of us have been forced to adopt similar survival strategies. Reflect on, or look in your journal at, your own list of survival strategies from your reflection in chapter 2. Do you notice any patterns with what you saw growing up and what you do today?

Take a breath here, if you need it. Stretch. Have some water. If you'd like, find something you can touch that helps you soothe, support yourself, and regulate your nervous system as we prepare to talk about what it was like for you as a child.

Your childhood experiences are felt by your nervous system and your inner child(ren). And you might already know this, but if you have your own children, you may unknowingly put things onto them that don't really have anything to do with them and have everything to do with your own childhood wounds. Like, sometimes deep grief in parenting shows up as fear when parents obsessively hover over their children, holding on to them too tightly, and seeking to control their decisions and surroundings. If you have parts of you that try to shame you for that, make space for that shame and offer it compassion if it feels sincere. It can be really hard to teach yourself a new way to be when it wasn't shown to you and the pain continued being passed down—like in Aiyana's story, where patterns of violence were learned and passed down generationally, stemming from deep ancestral grief and pain.

How do you give something you were never given? How do you do something if it's never been modeled to you? My answer to this is, it's still possible. Because love is within you already. Your Self-energy is love, and knows how to love whether or not you had it as a child. I can't say it won't be an uphill battle. But you *do* have the innate ability to love. You have the capacity to love. You were born with it. Find it by channeling your open heart. Take the risk to be vulnerable with receiving your own love, and the love of others. To the part of you carrying a sense of hopelessness around love—know that all is not lost. Your own Self-energy, or soul, can be that parent you never had. It can be that support you never saw. Because love is a part of every human's foundational nature and is your "default" mode, even when you feel you don't know how to do it.

It's important to delve in and explore the connections in your childhood story and consider how the historical trauma of your family's lineage has influenced the burdens you all carry and has incited intergenerational trauma. Don't worry, we're going to do it together.

Your Childhood Experiences

You probably had a mix of ups and downs in your childhood. Looking back, you might remember things that you appreciated about it and things you didn't. Maybe you remember your childhood as one big struggle because of things you saw happening in your home, how you were treated in school, or how you felt othered in spaces, including society. Maybe there were moments where you felt connected to family and times you didn't. Or maybe you never felt connected to your family at all. I think it's important to get a sense of what being a child was like for you—to reflect on your oldest burdens and the parts of you that've been around the longest trying to protect you. Let me ask you, what was it like for you growing up?

I invite you to start thinking about what you remember of your childhood. It can be your earliest memories or whatever organically surfaces. Don't worry if you don't remember all the details of your childhood. You might have clear memories or you might not remember much at all. Please know that what you know is good enough. Your vivid childhood memories may fade, but the energy of the past can still be passed down instead of stories and can stay trapped in your body. It will make its presence known to you somehow through the nervous system and body through rapid heart rate, increased respiration, tension in your muscles, chronic pain, and other ways. Trust what you know.

Dr. Frank Anderson, lead trainer of IFS, says that the parts of us carrying burdens live in our brains and express themselves through dysregulated channels in our nervous system when they're activated.[27] This means your nervous system and body will always tell the story of your painful past, even when you don't remember it all. Issues like chronic pain, intrusive thoughts about your childhood, and recurring dreams can all be signs of some emotional wounding needing your attention and the imprint of trauma inside you.

I want to reassure you, there's nothing wrong with you if you can't remember your entire childhood. Sometimes you might not remember because you have parts trying to protect you from the truth, especially when you had many painful moments as a kid. Saving yourself from remembering can be a way to avoid reliving your past hurt. And avoidance can be a powerful coping tool that keeps you from having to see, name, or own what is—even when it's coming from a part of you getting in the way of your remembering. The parts of you carrying the burden of avoidance and bypassing are usually trying to keep you from feeling your pain. And at the end of the day, that makes sense to me. Does it make sense to you why you'd want to avoid feeling your feelings?

Like frostbite, you don't feel the pain of your frozen hands until you thaw. It's when you're thawing that you begin to feel the pain of your frostbite—when you *allow* yourself to feel the feeling of your frostbite. You're going to need to feel through your grief, rage, and shame, in small doses, without being entirely overwhelmed, but you'll need to feel it all. And don't get me wrong, the goal isn't for you to relive old painful memories to retraumatize yourself in the name of healing. Your healing journey is more about facing and witnessing the parts of you carrying burdens, and then befriending and gaining the trust of these parts of you so that you can trust yourself better. It's about reclaiming and reconnecting with yourself, your ancestors, and your community, while releasing all the cultural, legacy, and personal burdens troubling you that may have also lingered for generations.

But before any real releasing can occur, you'll need to fully witness the burdens you're carrying. You witnessing your inner world is everything. The parts of you carrying these burdens will not release them until they're fully seen and acknowledged by you. Fortunately (and unfortunately), you know intuitively when you're trying to rush the healing process and bypass what's important for you to know about the burdens you carry. Seeing yourself is meaningful because it helps to heal the times in the past where you weren't seen. To dismiss your feelings or to hide from your emotions is invalidating yourself once more, unintentionally repeating cycles of abandonment. Seeing yourself really matters. Not because you can undo the past, but because you can stop perpetuating it when you witness your pain and tend to it.

That said, let's begin to witness more of your legacy burdens, attachment wounding, and intergenerational trauma, excavating parts of your story as you move deeper through your healing journey. If you're open to it, I'd like you to reflect on questions around your legacy.

REFLECTION PRACTICE:
Family Legacy

Step 1: Begin going inside yourself. Trust what comes up without thinking too deeply and getting in your head about it. Ask your heart first and wait for the answer. You're welcome to add to your answers if more comes up later for you. In the meantime, I'd like you to use this exercise as one small way to begin trusting what you have to say without overthinking, doubting, and judging. Just simply attune to yourself, notice what comes up, and jot it down. Are you ready? Let's see what's there.

- Who was influential to you growing up?

- What did you learn about authority as a child?

- How were boundaries set in your family? Were they respected or violated?

- What were the family secrets you held inside?

- How was conflict resolved in your family growing up? How did your caregivers fight?

- Did your caregivers withhold love from you when they were angry? If they did, what was that like for you? What did you learn about love and anger?

- If love was withheld from you as a kid, how has that affected your ability to show and receive love?

- How did you learn to trust (or not trust) yourself as a child?

- What did you have to do to receive love and acceptance from your family? Was love conditional?

Step 2: Take some time to write all that naturally comes up for you. When you have your answers, I invite you to consider how all of this impacts your relationships and your ability to show up in them. Think of the relationships you've had in all areas of your life. You can start in chronological order, or however works best. And be curious.

- How do your painful past memories and emotional wounds affect how you are with others? (For example, do you show up with armor, guarding your heart?)

- Do you project your pain onto others?

- Do you feel scared of getting close to others, letting them see you, or intensely fear their rejection and being vulnerable?

- Or do you feel like you often eagerly jump into relationships, hold tightly, or have a lot of intense emotions right from the start?

When your painful past interferes with how you're able to connect with others, the people who harmed you are energetically in the room with you. Rather than giving yourself and others the opportunity for a clean slate, your pain lingers and you may find yourself misdirecting it or projecting it onto others. Remember when I talked in chapter 3 about how your brain processes every experience from the bottom to the top and compares it with old experiences? And that your inner alarm systems go off when someone or something feels eerily familiar to your past wounding? Well, there's a reason for that. Let's rewind back to your nervous system in childhood.

As your nervous system started developing in infancy, it learned to perceive safety or danger (or a little of both) in your environment. As a child, feeling cared for by your caregivers brings a sense of safety to your nervous system. A sense of safety in your nervous system facilitates secure attachment and trust in your caregivers. But not everyone has the privilege of growing up with parents who felt safe and accepting. And sometimes, even when your caregivers *are* caring at heart, they might be overworked, depleted, depressed, anxious, and angry trying to survive and make a living in a system that perpetuates capitalism, racism, and ableism. Or you might've grown up separated from your parents because they lived in a different country, trying to work to provide for your family, and you grieve lost time with them.

Your caregivers may not have had the emotional reserves to care for you in the ways you needed, as much as their hearts were in the right place to do so. And it may have caused grief in your life, lack of safety, and attachment wounding. You might also struggle with some conflicting feelings of anger and tenderness toward your caregivers; it can feel incredibly difficult when someone you love has also betrayed you.

Maybe you were neglected emotionally or physically, or both, or maybe you've been emotionally, physically, or sexually abused all while your caregivers also showed you some care. If there are parts of you holding conflicting feelings toward your caregivers, know that it's okay to make space for compassion toward them without surrendering your own truth. Their behaviors toward you were probably learned, part of the intergenerational trauma of your lineage and the impact of trying to survive the inequitable systems they were a part of, all while carrying cultural, legacy, and personal burdens. Let yourself be where you are, and be with those polarizing feelings if you have them. Living within a racist and oppressive system is heartwrenching, and the greatest pain is often felt when you don't feel like you belong in your home or family either.

Let's take a pause. When you're ready, think about this really important question: *Have you ever felt safe in your life?*

Let the question sink in. Sometimes when you grow up not feeling entirely safe, you adjust and become accustomed to this unsafe feeling. Living with tension and a sense of danger and distrust becomes your baseline, and it can feel like you don't know anything else. And you never really know that you're missing out (or missed out) on a sense of safety until you actually begin to feel safe. You may see others experiencing safety or you might finally meet someone you can trust, be close to, and feel seen by. Then, it dawns on you that feeling safe is what you've been missing pretty much your whole life.

And it isn't that stress when you're a child is a terrible thing. Some stress is known to create resilience and a sense of confidence that you're able to overcome obstacles. We can benefit from stress in small doses. But we don't want to be overwhelmed with stress, because that's what creates traumatic stress. It's not only what happens to you that renders you powerless and leaves an imprint in your brain and nervous system, but it's even more a lack of support *afterward* that leads to traumatic stress. And as I've shared before, having support may not mitigate the traumatic stress of ongoing experiences of racism and oppression because they are enforced by larger systems that need decolonizing. Researchers have found three types of stress in childhood. Let me name them, as they each have their own effects on how we process a stressful event and whether or not it ends up being cataloged as "traumatic" in the future.

Three Types of Stress in Childhood

Stress can cause great harm when you're perceiving threat for too long or when you're left alone to fend for yourself, unable to make sense of what's happening. The three main types of stress in childhood are positive stress, tolerable stress, and toxic stress.

Positive stress is a short-term burst of stress (and a brief increase in heart rate) that's resolved with support and attunement from your caregivers (with whom you're able to co-regulate and restore a calm nervous system). As you experience these bouts of positive stress, your nervous system begins to develop healthy (and instinctual) self-regulation tools for returning to a calm, relaxed state when "threat" or "danger" has passed. As this happens, you can grow to feel confident and in control of your body.[28] An example of positive stress in youth would be if you ever had the "jitters" during your first day at school, and an encouraging grown-up showed up and provided a safe, compassionate presence.

Tolerable stress involves a onetime traumatic event. When you experience a frightening moment as a child and are met with attuned and supportive caregivers, your pain is witnessed and tended to and you're less likely to experience a posttraumatic stress response (especially if you're able to co-regulate and restore calm in your nervous system with your caregivers). An example of tolerable stress would be if a trusted adult behaved inappropriately with a child, and that child confided in their caregiver, who believed them right away and took all the necessary steps to protect the child, while continuing to create a safe space for the child to express and process all of their feelings about the incident.

Toxic stress, as I mentioned earlier, is a form of stress characterized by *ongoing exposure* to threat (real or perceived) and the *absence* of supportive and attuned caregivers or community—the type of stress that can lead to posttraumatic stress. If you don't have supportive and attuned caregivers to help you as a child, your nervous system has no one available to co-regulate with, and you're unable to self-regulate. These conditions create toxic stress in you as a child: experiencing ongoing painful events that result in fright, terror, or deep sadness, and the absence of care and support. Dr. Gabor Maté reminds us that children don't necessarily become traumatized because they're hurt, but because they're left alone with the hurt.[29]

What happens when you're betrayed, abused, or neglected growing up? What happens when the legacies of violence spill over onto the next generation and you've found yourself being hurt the same way your caregivers were? What happens when you don't feel safe in your childhood, causing disconnection and distrust of the people raising you? Your pain grows from the lack of connection, safety, and love from your caregivers. This is attachment trauma.

You might be wondering if you have attachment trauma, or you might already know that you do. Let me say a little more about attachment so that you can reflect on your own attachment style(s) and any attachment wounding you might have.

Getting to Know Your Attachment Styles

Attachment is understood as a felt sense of love and connection toward beings—seen and unseen. The world of psychology tends to discuss attachment just toward caregivers, but animism teaches that all of nature is living and has a soul too. And it's important to normalize attachment in this way for Black, Indigenous, and People of Color who have a deep kinship to land, ancestors and spirit guides, animals, trees, and all parts of nature.

With that understanding, let me explain the four different attachment styles that you can develop depending on the healthy or hurtful (a.k.a. traumatizing) environments you grow up in. I know the word "style" might sound a little odd, but I understand attachment styles as analogous to "attachment coping strategies." I see attachment styles as the way in which certain parts of you figured out how to emotionally cope as a kid. Attachment styles help create the template of how to do relationships when you've learned what to expect from them as a child.

Those who receive healthy support from their primary caregivers generally develop *secure attachment*, whereas those without security or safety in their child-caregiver relationship can develop one of three *insecure attachment* styles. And the thing about attachment styles is that we bring them with us into adulthood. We continue to use these same behaviors to adapt to our environments and in our relationships to maintain some sense of safety and control in our world. Especially when uncertainty may have meant danger, abuse, neglect, or loss for you as a kid. *Safety is a universal love language.* We can tell when we don't matter to people. We learn this early on in life, and many of us also get plenty of reminders from the world when othered. Feeling othered at home and like you don't matter can add to the tremendous grief and loneliness that precedes insecurity in our attachments with others.

First, let's talk about what it means to have secure attachment.

SECURE ATTACHMENT

The definition of a secure attachment between a child and their primary caregivers is one characterized by stability, consistency, trust, and the meeting of a child's physical and emotional needs from birth. The child is fed, clothed, and cleaned; is provided with a healthy and consistent routine; and receives emotional support and nurturing. Physical contact between a child and parent in a secure attachment involves safe touch, which, according to studies, could help their brains become in sync.[30] In a secure attachment, the caregivers will regularly

- express affection for their child;

- offer ample and consistent protection for their child, ensuring they're physically safe;

- build closeness and provide a space of acceptance for their child;

- be present for their child and have quality time together; and

- respect their child's body.

And let me be super clear, there's no such thing as perfect caregivers. Secure attachment is the goal, but we all have hiccups. And if you're a parent or caregiver in some capacity, you've probably faced some of your own imperfections. What's important is repairing after the hiccups between child and caregiver. Repair helps children not fear conflict. It also reduces shame and teaches children that their hearts and voices matter to their caregivers. For example, a parent who yelled at their child and later offered an openhearted apology, inviting the child to share their feelings and explore better ways to communicate, can still cultivate a secure attachment. You don't have to be a perfect caregiver. You just need to parent with intention, love, consistency, and consideration. This makes for secure attachment.

Attunement is the foundation of a secure attachment, and it's created through brain cells in all human beings called *mirror neurons*. These special neurons enable you to perceive and imitate the facial expressions of others, allowing you to intuitively experience someone else's energy just by looking at them. Can you remember seeing a baby who smiled when you smiled? And cooed when you spoke? As an infant, mirror neurons were responsible for your being able to reflect back the facial expressions and mouth movements of your caregivers. Some neuroscientists believe mirror neurons can help you interpret other people's emotions and intentions and can signal whether you're experiencing closeness or disconnection with someone. The mirror neurons in your brain helped you as a child to instinctually gauge your caregiver's emotional availability and how equipped they were to attune to you.

Now let's explore the three insecure attachment styles.

INSECURE ATTACHMENT

Insecure attachment is created when a child *does not* experience healthy emotional responsiveness or have their needs met consistently by the people raising them. This doesn't necessarily mean the caregivers aren't physically present (though many times they are not); insecure attachments can also be formed if the caregiver is anxious and puts their anxiety on to their child, or is in an abusive relationship and operating from a body in survival mode much of the time. If your caregivers were unable to connect with you as a child from a calm, grounded body and mind, your mirror neurons would've energetically communicated this disconnection to you and you'd likely feel insecure and fearful.

If your caregivers struggled with a dysregulated nervous system (maybe one that was constantly agitated or in fight, flight, freeze, or shutdown mode), your nervous system as a child would have also naturally become dysregulated in similar ways. You learn to regulate your body as a child based on how you see your caregivers regulating themselves.[31]

The three main types of insecure attachment that develop in childhood are dismissive-avoidant, anxious-preoccupied, and fearful-avoidant. As you read about the insecure attachment styles, I'm curious about which you recognize in yourself (and maybe in your caregivers). Let's start with dismissive-avoidant attachment.

Dismissive-avoidant attachment. This attachment style can be thought of as "extreme self-reliance" and mistrust of others. If the dismissive-avoidant attachment style resonates with you, you might notice you often feel guarded and reluctant to be vulnerable around others, mostly depending on yourself to meet your own needs. When you consider, from an internal family systems perspective, how some parts of you do things to try to protect you, it's safe to say that the urge to avoid is a strategy of protecting. And it would be important to ask yourself what you're avoiding and protecting yourself from. Your motto would probably be: "I can't depend on others to do things; I have to do them myself." You might find yourself keeping people at arm's length to avoid getting too close to them. You probably avoid being seen. Maria Alejandra, whose story you read in chapter 4, exhibited this attachment style when she chose emotionally unavailable men to date, unconsciously trying to avoid a real, deeper love.

Anxious-preoccupied attachment. This attachment style is characterized by a significant fear over the loss of connection or being rejected. If you have an anxious-preoccupied attachment style, you might find yourself in constant fear of losing a partner or close relationships. You may find that you deeply desire connection with others, but also depend too much on them to meet your needs and possibly even to "define" you. This attachment style can lead to parts of you that people please for approval or acceptance, or to avoid conflict and loss. Your motto would probably be: "Please love me and never leave. Sacrifice everything for me."

Fearful-avoidant attachment. This third style of insecure attachment involves going back and forth between wanting or seeking closeness, and fearing it or pushing it away. If this style resonates, you might find yourself conflicted with an internal push-and-pull between desiring connection with others and feeling terrified of the vulnerability of being seen. You might notice a polarization of longing to receive love and also trying to avoid it. Your motto would probably be: "See me, don't see me. Love me, don't love me. Help me, don't help me. Stay with me, leave me alone."

Do any of these attachment styles sound like yours? Sometimes more than one might resonate. Is there anything missing here that you'd like to add about how *you* experience your attachment styles? Think of the people who raised you. Do you get a sense of what their attachment styles were when you were young? The attachment styles we display were likely influenced by our caregivers' attachment styles, with unhealthy or insecure ones oftentimes leading to legacies of generational attachment trauma.

Let's take a breath here if it feels right. There's much more ahead to take in, and I want to make sure you give yourself a pause before you continue. I want to remind you to tend to your heart and care for yourself in all the ways you need. When you're ready, let's do some practice.

If you're feeling open to it, let's begin to explore possible legacies of attachment trauma. I invite you to consider your caregivers' childhood experiences and how their upbringing impacted yours. And once your reflection feels complete, take a moment for pause. Consider your childhood needs that weren't met.

JOURNALING PRACTICE:
My Unmet Needs

Step 1: I invite you to take out your notebook or a piece of paper to do a bit of reflective journaling. I want you to explore within yourself which childhood needs, if any, were unmet. Write what feels best and natural for you; there's no limit. This can be written in the form of a bulleted list or free-write. Trust what organically comes up for how you want it to look. You might say:

- I was not held or hugged as a child.

- I was often told or felt I was "too much" and a burden to my family.

- My caregivers never told me they were proud of me or complimented me on things.

- My caregivers didn't support or understand me.

- No one spent time with me as a kid.

- My caregivers made me hug family members I didn't feel comfortable with.

- My caregivers were hard on me about my grades and would yell and criticize me when I got grades they didn't think were good enough.

Step 2: Consider what kind of caregiver you needed back then. After you've done this, think about how you can meet these needs for yourself in adulthood. What does that look like?

Examples might include:

- I wasn't always hugged as a child, but I can give myself the safe touch I've always wanted.

- People may have believed I was "too much," but what I have to say is important, and it's okay for me to be myself.

- I was never really told by my caregivers how they felt about me, but I can remind myself that I am proud of all I've accomplished and see how hard I've tried.

- I may not have been seen the way I needed to be seen as a kid, but I am learning to see myself and appreciate me.

- I may not have received my caregiver's attention and support growing up, but I am building community and friends who are happy to offer love and care to me—and I deserve to be loved.

- I was asked to hug people against my will as a child, but now as an adult I am able to ask others to respect my physical boundaries and I continue learning to practice this. I can advocate for myself more now.

- Even though I was shamed by my caregivers about my grades not being perfect, I know now that my grades do not define me or reflect my capabilities. I am enough because I am inherently valuable.

As you consider the painful messages you received growing up, how you were loved or not loved, let's deepen our discussion on attachment trauma.

Attachment Trauma

Attachment trauma is the deep rupture of connection to all that was important to you—people, land, etcetera. One form of attachment trauma is developmental trauma, the unhealthy relational and emotional development that occurs when a child does not experience safety, trust, or a secure bond with their primary caregivers in their earliest years. If a caregiver is unable to consistently meet their child's emotional and physical needs or is perpetrating abuse and neglect, attachment trauma is the result.

Sometimes attachment wounding starts when you're an infant and can't talk or fully remember, like when children are exposed to violence and traumatic moments or intense environments before they're able to understand the world and before they even have language. We call this *preverbal and preconscious trauma*. The environments you grow up in have energetic fields, tension, and ambience. If the energy in your environments at a young age was tense, you might've internalized this.

One factor that pertains to attachment trauma has to do with implicit and explicit memory. All your experiences before the age of two are registered in your brain as implicit memory. After the age of two, your experiences are registered as explicit memory.[32] As an infant or toddler relying on implicit memory, you can't comprehend all that's happening around you, but your body *does* internalize the energy of abuse, lack of attunement, and abandonment around you. This leads to preverbal and preconscious trauma in your body. Preverbal and preconscious trauma usually shows up first in the form of sensations in the body, especially when the trauma happens before you developed language. It then influences your emotions, and eventually forges the story you tell yourself about your experiences. If you ever feel sensations or pain in the body that tends to surface regularly or during stressful times, it's something worth noting and being curious about. Next time you notice these bodily sensations, see if there are any images, words, or feelings attached to closeness with caregivers or family members. Hear the story and the strong feelings these sensations carry.

Legacies of Attachment Trauma

Insecure attachment styles can be passed down from generation to generation. This is a *legacy of attachment trauma*, and is part of the intergenerational and complex trauma that affects Communities of Color. One example of a legacy of attachment trauma would be if your caregiver used shame as a tool for parenting you, and you went on to become an adult who feared being vulnerable and continued the cycle of shaming others, including loved ones and children. I'm thinking of Aiyana, Dakota, and Malia's story as a prime example. We know that Aiyana's mother experienced and passed down a legacy of attachment trauma to Aiyana, who parented her daughters with similar attachment wounding fueled by intergenerational trauma.

Attachment trauma, and the painful things you think about yourself because of it, become legacy and personal burdens. Legacies of attachment trauma also include all the burdens that are held around colonization; ecocide (deliberate destruction of natural environments by humans, which can lead to the cultural genocide of the people who call it home and endanger the animals of that habitat); displacement from your homeland; genocide; enslavement; and loss of connection with your ancestors and spirit guides as kinship to roots, land, and home—connections that are sacred to many Black, Indigenous, and People of Color. These are also necessary to unburden and release when healing from complex posttraumatic stress. We bleed onto future generations when we're parenting and relating to others through the same attachment patterns our elders and ancestors needed for their own survival back then.

The beautiful thing is that it's never too late to feel secure attachment with someone, and developing a secure attachment with someone can help *you* be more loving to yourself too. In internal family systems, your core Self is believed to have the power to be that loving energy to you, and can help tend to your parts that fear connection. One way to do this is through reparenting your inner child by being the parent to yourself that you wish you had. Remember, as I said in chapter 5, your Self is a resource to the parts of you needing love.

In the next practice, I invite you to think about what you learned growing up. How you learned to be, and what you learned to do from your caregivers. Once you do that, I'd like you to reflect on the qualities, beliefs, rules, and burdens you've inherited from previous generations. Feel free to start slow, with less emotionally charged things, and then go deeper into the patterns you notice from your caregivers that are within you.

REFLECTION PRACTICE:
Exploring My Intergenerational Patterns

This practice is inspired by a psychodrama practice I learned years ago.

Step 1: On a blank page, draw vertical lines from top to bottom to create a column for every one of your primary caregivers. Leave enough space in each column for at least ten or so responses. Inside each column, write a list of adjectives that describe that caregiver, including both positive and negative descriptors (e.g., cold, distant, rigid, warm, abusive, funny, generous, angry, submissive, controlling, anxious, dismissive, cheerful, unhappy).

Step 2: When you're done filling in each column, write the implicit and explicit rules you remember growing up, and who said them (e.g., "Don't cry in front of people"—Dad; "Don't talk to people about your problems"—Mom; "Don't ask for help, just do it yourself"—Abuela; "Don't show vulnerability or weakness"—Nana).

Step 3: Once you've written everything down, circle the adjectives of your caregivers that you *see in yourself*. How many of their adjectives do you see in your own behaviors and thought processes?

Step 4: Finally, circle the rules you still practice yourself, or parent with if you have children. Reflect on what you've written and gauge:

- What rules have you upheld in your own life and/or when parenting?

- What patterns do you notice? And how do you feel about these patterns?

Take a breath here, if you need, before we move into the important topic of how to begin breaking these intergenerational patterns.

Breaking Generational Curses

Abuse patterns and legacy burdens passed down in your family are sometimes referred to as *generational curses* (particularly the dynamics that get in the way of you and your family being your best Selves). It's the stuff you didn't want and never asked for, but got anyway. Generational curses, like intergenerational trauma, are the patterns of abuse that are transferred to every generation because there's little to no awareness around the harm being perpetuated. There's no healing happening and just more of the same. And as I shared before, the legacy burdens in your family come from historical trauma and cultural legacy burdens being perpetuated from the larger system you're raised in.

A generational curse may exist, for instance, when you're often finding yourself in abusive relationships and your family carries a pattern of abusive relationships. Or when you're parenting your children in the same harsh ways you were parented. Or seeing the pattern of emotional neglect in your family and finding yourself dating emotionally unavailable people. When you hear others use the term "generational curses," know that they're speaking interchangeably of the intergenerational trauma and transmission of legacy burdens throughout your lineage. Here's how these generational curses and legacy burdens can show up in your family.

Burden of scarcity: The burden of scarcity is that deep sense of not having enough. I find there's grief attached to this. Carrying a burden of scarcity is a reaction from the trauma of poverty, attachment wounding, and isms. Remember Aiyana's story? Aiyana struggled often with the feeling of not ever having enough. Besides growing up not having enough financially, she also grew up not having enough love. Sometimes we tend to think scarcity is solely about money. But when you've had a childhood full of lack, your brain and nervous system adjust to anticipate scarcity in all areas of your life (so you can predict it and mitigate harm around the surprise of scarcity or loss). When you're used to not having your needs met growing up, you grow to believe scarcity is the norm. And eventually, when you're older, the burden of scarcity shows up in your relationships and affects your worldview. There's never enough love, never enough time, never enough money (and let's be real, sometimes there really isn't enough money when capitalism exploits Black, Indigenous, and People of Color). But then anxiety, fear, and shame come knocking at your door, telling you that *you* aren't enough. And now it's personal and directed at your spirit.

Do you carry a burden of scarcity? Sometimes it can feel like an emptiness inside, where you're constantly trying to fill a void by chasing more, asking for more, and doing more—all to no avail. Because you've been conditioned to believe, through cultural legacy burdens and familial legacy burdens, that you're lacking. And sure, maybe your abundance doesn't look like the intergenerational wealth of others. But the love from your ancestors and the community waiting to celebrate you and all the possibility for your healing is abundant. Your power is abundant. The more you release this burden of scarcity, the more you can make room for abundance how *you* see and feel it.

Holding the family secrets: Have you ever had to keep a secret in your family, or about your family? Maybe you held a loved one's secret of sexual abuse by another family member, or perhaps you were the survivor of sexual abuse by a loved one. Maybe you couldn't bear "telling on" your loved one, or maybe you were told not to talk to anyone inside or outside of your family. Or heartbreakingly, maybe you weren't believed by your family when you *did* say something. I'm also wondering if you've ever had to hold a secret for a caregiver from another caregiver. Or from the rest of your family (e.g., if you had to hold the secret of an affair, abusive behavior, or addiction of a parent). It can feel really lonely, especially as a child, to hold your family secrets. It can certainly bring up grief and rage as you deal with the loss of normalcy and childhood innocence. And it chips away at your ability (or desire) to trust others, creating a harrowing sense of insecurity.

If you've had to hold a secret growing up, or are still holding one, I want you to know that you can put it down when you're ready. The burden of secrecy is heavy. You can tell someone you trust who can hold it with you. And hold you, too. This burden doesn't belong to you. Like you, I've also had to hold secrets. When I was a child and for a long time after, I held the secret of sexual abuse by a family member whom I trusted and loved and looked up to. And it was hard to make sense of, because as a child you usually believe everything that happens to you is because of you. I remember the first time I disclosed to a cousin what had happened to me. This was the first time in years I ever said anything to anyone. I believed I was bad. And it was clear that I was carrying a burden of shame and blamed myself for the harm done to me. Because that's what kids do. They blame themselves and internalize the abusive behavior of others, believing they caused it. And when you suffer sexual betrayal from a loved one as a child, you want the abuse to stop but the love to remain. Sometimes you feel shame in still loving the person who abused you and shame if you don't want them to get in trouble. I never wanted him to get in trouble, I just wanted it to stop so I didn't have to live in fear anymore.

If you have a similar story, know that I'm sending love to you. Know that you don't have to be alone carrying this burden. And sadly, there are many like us in these shoes. Can I ask—what are you holding in your heart? Does an untold story live there? If it's okay, let's reach in.

REFLECTION PRACTICE:
Releasing an Untold Story

Be gentle and take your time with this. But if you're open to it, write this secret down and seal it tightly in a jar, or an envelope. Put it somewhere safe for when you're ready to open it up and share it with someone. Or simply open when you're ready and read it to yourself. Speak to yourself at the age you were, and offer your younger parts the love, encouragement, and advocacy you maybe wished you had back then. This is how you show up for yourself. It's you becoming your own champion and beginning to foster secure attachment with your Self. Give yourself the words you most needed back then. Show up for yourself in the scenes that come up for you around your pain, and do all that you wish had been done for you back then, now. This is what IFS calls a "do-over." You can't turn back the clock and undo what has already been done. But you *do* have the power to heal what needs to be healed around it. Slowly, at your own pace.

As we consider the burden of holding secrets, I'm reminded of how impaired boundaries in a family system can also be inherited through attachment wounds. We tend to replicate what we see from caregivers, and both diffuse and rigid boundaries can erode our felt sense of safety.

Inherited Faulty Boundaries

Boundaries are energetic, spiritual, physical, and emotional. They are how you know where you end and where another person begins. Boundaries serve to help you hold on to yourself and differentiate you from another. They are sometimes a resounding "yes," and other times a calm "no." They are the courage of truth telling when you've been coerced to hold family secrets, even when you upset people with that truth. When we inherit attachment wounds, however, we may have a hard time setting or maintaining healthy boundaries. This is due to what's called *trauma bonding* (feeling responsible, loyal, and bonded to someone who has abused you).

Sometimes trauma bonding makes it hard to set boundaries with family and others, especially if you've been indoctrinated to remain loyal at all costs. Loyalty can be valuable and necessary for our village to care for each other and look out for one another. *But loyalty without boundaries and accountability is harmful.* Trauma bonds tend to develop after you've repeatedly endured toxic stress (like physical, sexual, or emotional abuse and neglect) with a caregiver (or anyone) over a prolonged period of time whom you also depended on to keep you safe. On one hand, you've been deeply hurt by them. On the other hand, you may care about them and need them to survive if you're a child. And as you grow, you may feel sympathy for their pain. So rather than set boundaries with them, you might find yourself swallowing your words out of fear of making them feel guilty. But boundaries are important in preserving relationships (including the one you have with yourself). If you fear setting boundaries or get defensive when people set boundaries with you, it's likely because your attachment wounds tell you that boundaries are a rejection of you. But it's quite the opposite.

Clear boundaries are consistent, loving, open, and meant to empower your inner world and your external relationships. They're also necessary, in childhood and beyond. I can't emphasize that enough. If you didn't see people setting boundaries growing up, you're not going to learn how to set them. If boundaries were violated in your family, you're not going to really know how to stand by yours. If they were either too rigid or too fluid, your boundaries will also either isolate others or overextend.

And the thing is, your caregivers likely never taught you about boundaries because they were never taught to have them. When we consider the effects of historical trauma in your ancestral lineage, past pain taught your elders that they didn't have a right or power to advocate for themselves. And worse, standing up and speaking out led to harsh punishment or abandonment. Your elders may not have taught you to have a voice because they've taught themselves to be silent to survive.

Let's take a moment to take a deep breath if that feels right. Maybe close your eyes for a second to rest your lids. You've done a lot so far. Feel your heart beating and your breath connecting the outer world with your inner world. Notice if there are any parts of you needing your attention right now before we continue, and let them know you're there for them. I want to remind you that your soul is deserving of belonging and safety. Allow yourself to take that in if you can.

To Wrap It All Up...

So much to glean, love. And I'm thankful you've journeyed this far with me. As you spend more time exploring and being with your legacy burdens from intergenerational trauma rooted in historical trauma, you gain more clarity. Over time, as you feel clearer about these generational patterns, be curious about what you need to release the legacy burdens and shift the energy of multigenerational trauma to posttraumatic resilience and intergenerational healing for you, your family, and your community. You cannot do this alone. And you can reunite with your ancestral wisdom. Many of us long and thirst for that. Reconnecting with your ancestors, known and unknown, is a meaningful way to reclaim what was stolen from you. I'm really looking forward to spending more time with you as you get to know your ancestors more in the next chapter. Being in connection with your ancestors helps you to stay connected with yourself. It fights against the cultural legacy burden of individualism when we realize that we're never truly alone and our hearts beat with the sacred medicine of our ancestral love. In the meantime, rest your spirit, and co-regulate with nature and people you trust. Be gentle with yourself and send care to all your parts if it feels sincere. When you're ready to do some ancestral work together, I'll be here. See you soon.

CHAPTER 9

Third Empowerment Step: Access the Energy of Your Ancestors' Wisdom

We've reflected on the many ways that cultural and legacy burdens have hurt your family for generations. How cultural and legacy burdens inflicted on your family come from the pain of historical trauma and trying to survive in a structurally racist and oppressive system. Dr. Bruce Perry studied with the Maori people and learned that the Maori culture understood depression, anxiety, addiction, and other mental health struggles to be deep-rooted issues of disconnection with community and within.[33] He also learned that ancestors knew the importance of connectedness and the harm in exclusion. Historical trauma is ancestral trauma. And historical trauma like colonization and enslavement can disrupt connection within communities, creating a cultural genocide. These wounds of historical trauma have left imprints on successive generations, in your elders and you. While you may carry the painful legacies of your ancestors' trauma, you also carry their resilience. Your ancestors' energy lives within you, like their DNA, courage, and intuition. Regaining the spirit of your ancestors as you reclaim your healing can help you embody more of your ancestral wisdom.

Your ancestors, known and unknown, love you. They've been watching you grow and are rooting for you. They journey the world with you and they can be great guides to turn to and help you with those hard decisions when you're feeling lost.[34] They've carried both legacy burdens and legacy resources. And you don't just inherit their burdens from historical trauma; you receive their ancestral intuitive gifts and resilience as well. You're already connected to the spirit of your ancestors; it just looks different for each of us.

Do you ever feel curious about the courage of your ancestors? I've wondered what it was like for my ancestors to raise their children or be in relationships after having gone through profound grief, having had their resources and spiritual practices stolen and their land colonized, and having endured merciless relational trauma. How did they risk trusting again after all they'd been through? I wonder about the tears they shed and the ones they hid, even from themselves. I wonder about the dreams they were robbed of and the villages of support they were deprived of. I wonder how generations of children grew to imperfectly parent from legacies of trauma while trying their hardest to do better and break cycles of violence.

And I wonder what the trauma cycles looked like. How much of their own coping mechanisms they mistakenly believed were their personality, rather than traumatic stress. I even wonder how they held on to their strength and resilience with the loss of a sense of safety and loss of all they knew. Did they feel they could ever belong again? My hunch is, if you and I are here, all hope wasn't lost. Because despite the hate and dehumanization your ancestors suffered, their spirits could never be broken. Neither can yours.

Now, there might be a part of you that believes this ancestral work is woo-woo stuff. Sometimes connecting to our ancestors (known and unknown) can feel so unattainable, and even weird, if you've been taught by religious groups and other people to erase your ancestors or distance yourself from them. And I get it; considering many of us have had our spiritual practices and traditions hijacked, shamed, or even co-opted, you might naturally have some reservations. Or maybe you notice you're protecting yourself from your ancestors, feel mad at them, or fear that they don't know you and you don't have any ancestral guides. All of your feelings and the parts that may be coming up for you matter. Feel into what you need to give yourself the permission to be open to connecting to your ancestors and to hold any other feelings too.

Would you be willing to try something new and connect with your ancestors? Please know that your ambivalence and reservations are welcome to journey with you as you learn and practice more. It's okay to be unsure and have conflicting feelings. Remember to take what works for you, and to leave what doesn't. I'm confident and trusting that you know what's best for your inner world and what helps you feel most connected to your lineage and community. And you can always come back and try the practices in this chapter again if you're ever more curious.

On the other hand, you may already be engaging in an ancestral spiritual practice. That's great too. Mainstream healing practices for folks in the global majority have not included what is being proven to be a vital part of healing for many Communities of Color that have ancestral lineages of trauma and legacy burdens. That also includes other energies in our healing that can connect us even more to the spirit of nature, all living beings (e.g., animals, plants) around us, and the earth too, allowing us to co-regulate with nature. And it's becoming more and more evident that rebuilding a relationship with your ancestors means:

- helping you know yourself with a deep, spiritual lens

- feeling more supported and protected by your ancestors' energy

- increasing your sense of belonging and power

- continuing to inherit their legacy resources and wisdom

- strengthening connection to your intuition

You may feel disconnected from your ancestors, known and unknown. But they are very much alive within you. Your ancestral ties run deep and no one can take that away, even when they've tried many times before. Let this speak life back into your spirit when it feels like it's withering. I've come to believe that our ancestors' whispers are part of our intuition. That when we're feeling lost and trying to find our way, our ancestral wisdom reminds us to lead with courage, with intention, and to remember who we are, unburdened. Our intuition being led by an ancestral whisper can feel like that sudden inner voice saying, "Don't go down that road" or "Don't trust this person; something doesn't feel right." Some might say it's like your sixth sense.

And to be clear, the purpose of ancestral work isn't to singlehandedly heal your ancestors. You alone cannot heal your ancestral lineage; your ancestors that are well in spirit in your lineage can help do that. Dr. Daniel Foor's book *Ancestral Medicine: Rituals for Personal and Family Healing* encourages learning about your four primary bloodlines to find the ancestors that are well in spirit (your ancestral guides). If you're curious, I recommend the work of ancestral medicine practitioners to help you deepen the practice on finding ancestral guides that are well in your lineage. In the meantime, the goal here for the third empowerment step is to practice ancestral reverence, connect with the spirit of your ancestors, and reach into their legacy resources so that you can call upon them for guidance and strength. They can be such an integral part of your healing, sense of support, and sense of identity.

If you're feeling open to renewing and fortifying a connection with your ancestors, let's channel them. First, I invite you to pay a visit to them and see who shows up to meet you on the journey. As you do this practice more, other ancestors may also come forward to meet you. See how you feel in their presence. Know that you can set energetic boundaries with any ancestral energy that doesn't feel good to you by asking them to keep their distance, and ask for another to come forward.

MEDITATION PRACTICE:
A Visit with My Ancestors

(You can download an audio recording of this practice at http://www.newharbinger.com/49319.)

Step 1: In all the ways you feel comfortable, I invite you to take a deep breath in and allow your heart to open. Slowly release any tension you feel stored in your body as you exhale.

Step 2: Now, journey inside yourself for a moment. Visualize yourself in a place that brings safety to your heart. When you're there and when you're ready, invite an ancestor to come to you. Wait for them. You might even ask for an ancestor from a particular lineage of yours to come forward. When your ancestor appears, do what intuitively comes to you to greet them. This might be the first time you've met this ancestor, or you might already be familiar with them. If more than one shows up, feel free to spend the time together as you all see valuable.

Step 3: Soak in this time with them. When the time feels right for you both, ask them the questions living in your heart.

Step 4: Be with them. Reflect on what you might need from them. It's okay to ask for their support. It's okay to open your heart to them. It's okay to trust. How can they support you through what you've been going through lately? What do they want you to know about them? What do you want them to know about you? What do you need to feel more connected to them? What needs to happen to bring you closer?

Step 5: Slowly inhale and steadily exhale, releasing any tension you notice in your body. If it feels right, ask them to cover you with love. Ask them to restore and empower your spirit with courage and peace. Ask for their protection. Hear their responses to you and visualize the love they offer you flowing through your veins. You carry their power.

Step 6: If you're willing, make a commitment to your ancestors to connect with them more often. You can make a daily or weekly practice. Start with what feels right. Know that you can connect with your ancestors whenever you'd like. If this is your first time, rest assured it's only the beginning of many more reunions. It's true that you honor your ancestors when you begin to liberate yourself. Your ancestors can be important guides in this work if you are open to their help. Call on them any time you feel disempowered. They will support you in the ways you allow.

Step 7: When that feels complete, express your gratitude for their connection and begin making your way back to your body. Take another deep breath as you return from your ancestral journey. Feel your body present in the space you're in. Breathe in community. Breathe out isolation. You're not alone.

How was that for you? Be gentle with yourself and tender with your heart. Journal about your experience with your ancestor(s) and write down any messages you'd like to hold on to. As you go about your day, remember to offer your heart the love they've given you.

Sometimes, during the most challenging moments of your life, it can feel lonely. You might struggle finding community, or sometimes people you love cannot show up for you in the ways you need because they have their own struggles. When you're going through something that feels difficult and you're needing a reminder of your power, this journal practice might help uplift your spirit.

JOURNALING PRACTICE:
My Ancestors Root for Me

I invite you to envision your ancestors, known or unknown, rooting for you. It can be the ancestor(s) you've met before or others that naturally show up.

Step 1: Visualize yourself entering the world as an infant, being welcomed by your ancestors and other people you trust. See them happy that you were born. Take in the energy field of laughter and joy from the environment.

Step 2: Now see yourself in other scenes as you're growing. Envision your ancestors and all of the people you trust celebrating you in these different moments of your life. Hear them offering words of encouragement to you. Take your time with this and see what scenes come up for your organically. See your ancestors rooting for you in all of them.

Step 3: Now, if it feels right, envision them being at a difficult moment in your life. Feel them giving you strength and words of wisdom, and putting the energy of love and hope in the palm of your hand or in your heart. They know your tenacity and what you're made of, because you're cut from the same resilient cloth. When that feels complete and you're ready, thank them for showing up. You might also give them an offering at a later time.

As we explore the practice of offerings, I recommend creating a sacred space for your ancestral reverence. A designated place where you can talk to them and give them offerings (things you know they enjoy). This place of dedication can act like a portal connecting you to your ancestors. Remember the inner child altar exercise in chapter 6? This is one of the original ways elders from many cultures of the global majority have learned to give reverence and stay connected with ancestors and other protective guides and energies. If you're open to it (and haven't already done so), create an altar with things that represent the four elements: fire, earth, air, and water. If you know your protective guides, add something that represents them, like a picture, figurine or object (like the Orishá or other deities), symbol, material, or stone in the center of your altar. Let loose with your vision. Make it yours. You can add flowers, incense, crystals, books, art, and other offerings that feel right to help cultivate sacred energy. Remember that when you're being creative, you're channeling a quality of Self-energy.

Let's begin reflecting on the sacred elements (like fire, earth, air, and water) and the directions (east, west, north, and south). There's so much wisdom when we see how we interact with nature and the earth. IFS lead trainer Chris Burris said that "the elements go beyond language."[35] The elements can remind you of Earth's natural resources and your own inner nature, as the elements also represent your zodiac sign. Let's do a practice together to connect with the spirit of nature and use directions and elements in some internal reflection.

REFLECTION PRACTICE:
Being with the Elements and Directions

You can do this practice in multiple ways. You can turn your physical body as you turn toward each direction. Or you might just read along and reflect, or journal. See what feels right for you. Remember that you can always come back and do this exercise in a different way.

Step 1: Start in the east, as the sun rises there. Every day the sun rises in the east and sets in the west. It's consistent. The sun burns hot gas. The element of fire has the ability to both destroy and activate. Its flame can destroy toxins and can also awaken healing energy, like when you burn a candle or incense. Like the sun, how will you awaken? What does your soul long for?

Step 2: When you're ready, turn left to the west. In the west, you'll find water. Water is cleansing. It teaches you flexibility. It can transform to different states (liquid, solid, gas), yet at its core it remains the same. Water reminds you to go with the flow. And when water encounters barriers like boulders in the river stream, it moves around them. What do you learn from water? How can you further embody the flexibility of water? What do you need to help cleanse your spirit of the toxins in toxic stress?

Step 3: Next, turn to the north. In the north, you'll find wind (air). Here, you can connect with your ancestors. Your ancestors are like your North Star, giving you direction and guidance. Call on them when you'd like to connect.

Step 4: When you're ready, turn to the south. In the south, you honor the earth. If it's possible, ground yourself in the dirt and soil. If you're nearby a tree, remember where its roots connect. Reflect on the ways you can root yourself in your truth and authenticity.

Step 5: And finally, turn toward the center. The center symbolizes your spirit. It represents your Self. Feel into who you are when you're not carrying burdens. Breathe deeply. When you're ready, return to the present and notice where you are in time and space.

How was that for you? There's something so powerful about connecting with both your ancestors and your Self, being both ancestor-led and Self-led. Let's talk more about how you can call on your ancestors and deepen your connection.

Ancestral Invocation

You can use prayer, in whatever way that feels right to you, or any form of invocation to seek your ancestors. Ancestral work doesn't require religion, so find the way that feels right to call on them when you're wanting to connect. Your invocation can be a casual conversation, like a check-in, or a reaching out for protection. You can also use your invocation as a way to stay close with family members who have passed on. Sometimes I'll reach out to my *abuelita* or cousin who passed away and ask for guidance and protection with a problem that feels bigger than I can carry. And it helps me be with my grief for their loss, when I remember they're still a part of my life in a different way. How do you reach out to your ancestors? Two ways to connect are through signs and through dreams.

Ancestral spirit presence: Have you ever had that experience where you're asking for a sign from the universe, or your ancestors, and suddenly something happens that feels like divine intervention? Many times, the spirit of your ancestors comes in forms you don't even realize. It can show up as the butterfly that lands on your shoulder, or the bird that lands on your window when you're having a hard day and wishing things were easier. Sometimes the spirit of your ancestors can make its presence known in the form of a sudden gust of air, scents, a voice in your thoughts that isn't yours (not one that's attached to an emotion or concern that's yours— but more like a guiding voice), sounds, touch, or shadows that pass through your side view.

Connect with ancestors in dreams: I'm curious—how's your relationship with your dreams? Some folks with complex posttraumatic stress might have dreams that resemble intrusive memories or flashbacks, have lucid dreams, or not remember their dreams at all. I'm a big fan of dreams, as I've found there's so much information for us when we enter a sleep state and rapid eye movement. Sometimes people use dreams as a guide and as their warning system.

I encourage you to be more curious about your dreams. Do you keep a dream journal? It can be helpful to create a morning routine for yourself where you jot down your dreams when you wake. Dreams carry energy, symbolism, and healing potential.[36] You can find meaning in the symbolism of the scenes, feelings, words, messages, people, and animals that enter your dreams. Your ancestors can appear in your dreams to speak with you, giving you a message you didn't know you needed. You can also channel your ancestors through your dreams (and other family members who have passed on). If you're up for it, consider writing a letter to your ancestors and put it near your bed (or under your pillow), or speak to your ancestors out loud or in prayer or invocation before you sleep. Ask them that question you have, or share with them what you're holding in your heart. Create a dream ritual that includes your ancestors and that helps complement your healing.

Ancestral Guidance

As you continue your journey of connecting with ancestors and navigate systemic racism and oppression, ask for their support and lean into their legacy resources. When you minimize yourself, imagine your elders, ancestors, and the people you trust and feel supported by around you. Holding you. Surrounding you and protecting you in their collective energy field. Imagine them offering you words of love, encouragement, and affirmation. You might even offer yourself an affirmation that's rooted in your liberation and dignity. Your presence in the world is important. Your voice is important. Your words are important. Your fire, your passion, your intensity, your authenticity—they all add value to the work you do and the spaces you're a part of. Know that you have a right to take up space.

Your ancestral pillars will forever be there holding up your foundation. Recognize the truth and medicine of the collective power of the global majority. When you're feeling othered, and like an outsider to the world you live in, pause. Take a deep breath, close your eyes if it makes sense, and call on your ancestors to help you in the moments you feel scared. Call on them when you're unsure of how to show up in your fullness. Hear their affirmations of you. Feel their impenetrable protective shield around you. Feel into your own Self-energy and core wisdom too. Like lightning from the clouds to the land, envision the invigorating energy of connection between you and the ancestral plane. Your ancestors can hold your grief, fear, and rage with you. And they can also help you unburden it.

Unburdening, or releasing burdens, happens in layers—especially with complex trauma and the remnants of historical trauma in intergenerational trauma. Before we end this chapter, I'd like to share two unburdening practices that can help you slowly and safely release the burdens you've been carrying. Ideally, you've already gotten connected with a mental health professional for some of the deeper work (and if not, there's a list of resources at the back of the book to help you find your way).

GUIDED VISUALIZATION AND JOURNALING PRACTICE: Unburdening with Ancestors

(You can download an audio recording of this practice at http://www.newharbinger.com/49319.)

As you consider the cultural and legacy burdens you're carrying in your mind, body, and spirit, see how they show up for you.

Step 1: Go back to your journal and the practices in chapter 2 if you can't recall the cultural and legacy burdens you carry. See the burdens you're holding. Have you internalized racism and transphobia because of all the times you were called racial slurs or were misgendered? Do you often compete with family and friends because a part of you is afraid there isn't enough to go around for everyone? Are you feeling trapped in toxic relationships because you feel you don't deserve love?

Step 2: Be with whatever you notice coming up for you. You might need to be with it in doses if it ever gets overwhelming, and that's okay too. Befriending and witnessing your parts helps your healing. Notice what's happening in your body. If you don't notice anything right away, that's fine. Just scan your body for any tension, tightness, pressure, pain, or discomfort.

Step 3: Wherever you notice these coming up in your body, see if there are scenes, images, words, voices, or phrases that come with these body sensations.

Step 4: If it feels sincere, continue to extend curiosity to the parts of you coming up and get to know the burdens they carry. What isms have taken over your heart? What isms have your parts internalized, and what parts of you have risen in service to protect you from these isms and your own vulnerability?

Step 5: Continue to get to know the beliefs you've been holding about yourself that aren't yours, but what you've taken on living in an oppressive system. Ask your parts what they need to feel safe and trusting of you. Ask your parts if they'd be willing to release, little by little, some of the burdens they carry so that you can show up in your fullness—more authentically with family, friends, and relationships, and even more aligned to your culture. It's hard to live guarded every day. Putting up walls can be great protection, but it also closes you off from the love you're deeply longing for. The belonging you hunger for. And the peace your heart strives for.

Step 6: Consider the legacy burdens you carry that were inherited from your family, rooted in historical trauma. Where do these burdens live in your body? Witness anything and everything that feels right and that organically comes up around these burdens. Go at your own pace. Take your time to really befriend and witness what some of your parts have been holding. With an open heart, show them you care. When that truly feels complete, would you be willing to release some of these burdens to the sacred elements? Releasing burdens to the elements can be a form of shape-shifting these burdens from an energy of toxicity and pain to a different kind of energy that feeds the earth—like composting.

Step 7: You can do this unburdening practice in your mind or physically. If you'd like, write down these cultural and legacy burdens on a piece of paper (you can also include personal burdens) and prepare to release them to the elements.

Step 8: When you're ready, you can place the burdens in a fire, release them to the water to drift away or dissolve, bury them in the earth, or give them to your ancestors. As a team, you can all work together to dispose of them. See what feels most right for you. Whichever you choose, you can always invite your ancestors to help you handle the burdens and release them. Take your time releasing the burdens you want to release today. Know that you can come back and continue releasing the burdens that are wounding you over time. Sometimes we need to do this over and over to begin feeling more spaciousness inside, and more unburdened.

Step 9: When you're ready, invite back the qualities that feel important to you and that are *you* at your core, as well as any qualities you might need in the future. Who do you believe yourself to be, unburdened? Name and reclaim those qualities that became inaccessible because of the cultural, legacy, and personal burdens that polluted your internal world—from toxic stress in childhood to racism, homophobia, transphobia, oppression, xenophobia, other isms, and historical trauma. *Retrieve your soul.*

And lastly, I'm eager to share with you one last method to release toxic energy and unburden in an unconventional spiritual way.

CULTURAL CEREMONIAL PRACTICE:
Unburdening and Aura Cleansing with a "Limpia"

The shamanic practice called a "limpia" is a common ritual in Mexico, Mesoamerica, and the Caribbean for people carrying pain and distress in their bodies. The purpose of a limpia is to release the toxic energy you're holding in your body and contain it in another object that can be discarded. In a limpia, you use a raw egg and transfer the pain you're holding in your body into the egg, and throw it away afterward.

The egg is believed to be a symbol of life, and because of this it can absorb energy. Many shamans and healers in *curanderismo* use this ancient healing practice to remove toxic energy from a person who is sick and has been cursed and to help clear the chakras. (This includes someone who was given "the evil eye," or "mal de ojo," by a person who envies them and wishes them harm and loss.) This was a common practice in my family when "mal de ojo" was put on someone. They'd know when they suddenly fell ill or were suffering and felt unrecognizable to themselves.

You may already be familiar with this practice, or you might be learning about it for the first time. Here are the steps to follow when you're doing a limpia:

Step 1: Get a raw egg and wash it with salt water or Florida water (*agua Florida*, which is known to successfully cleanse the environment of harmful energy) and lemon juice. You might even say a prayer for protection while holding the egg or while putting it gently over a flame. You can say a prayer as you go through the steps, though it isn't necessary. You can also ask the African Orishá (or Òrìsà) or other protective guides you're connected with to help you during and after this releasing ceremony. If you feel called, you might even ask your ancestors to help protect you and ask for their blessing.

Step 2: When you're ready, begin rolling the uncooked egg on your forehead and all over your body with your dominant hand. Roll it like you would a muscle roller. Focus on any areas that stand out to you, either where you experience chronic pain or wherever you're feeling heavy and burdened. Roll for several minutes until it feels complete (without it cracking).

Step 3: Once you're done rolling the egg, express gratitude and reverence for the transfer of toxic energy you've been holding onto the egg. You can dispose of the egg in a small bag and take it to a place distant from your home (or space) that you rarely pass. The reason for this is to remain far removed from the egg that has absorbed the pain and energy of your burdens. Sometimes, if there's a shaman present, they might crack the egg open and read the egg to see what you've been carrying. For the sake of this practice, we'll keep it simple.

Step 4: After you've done this, burn sage to clear the energy field in your home or whatever space you're in. Don't forget to open your windows if you do this, as any remaining unwanted energy will need a way to leave your home. For extra cleansing, you can wipe down and mop the floors with Florida water. You can also take a warm bath with rose petals, which can relieve infection and increase circulation. Lastly, you can smudge your body with sage, palo santo, cedar, or sweetgrass. As good practice, please use an apothecary for these plant materials, get permission from the land, and express gratitude to the earth for the healing elements you're using.

Making this a regular ritual can help you connect with ancestral practices and shift the energy of burdens around. It's another way to call upon the ancestors, guides, and Earth's elements for your unburdening. I call on my own ancestors and the Orishá in Yorùbá (*Ifá*) tradition as protective guides, especially Changó and Ochún.

There are so many more ways for you to continue practicing connection with your ancestors, and many ways to release and unburden that are aligned to the cultural traditions of your ancestors. I invite you to research them. Seek them out. Customize your healing practice with the rituals of your family's culture(s).

To Wrap It All Up...

I'm really appreciating this time as we journey through this book together. You've opened your heart to reflecting on so many of the cultural, legacy, and personal burdens you (and your family) carry and their ties to historical trauma. In part III we talked about Aiyana, Dakota, and Malia's story and saw how intergenerational trauma and generational curses and legacies of attachment trauma played out in their lineage. You reflected on your own attachment styles and wounding, and maybe even noticed how they show up in your relationships today. You've also started exploring your own connection to your ancestors, known and unknown, and your relationship with nature and the elements. Regaining connection to the spirit of your ancestors can bring such a sense of support, community, and identity and helps deepen your own intuition. You didn't just inherit ancestral burdens; you've also received their heirlooms. And the more you deepen your ancestral connection and ritual, the more you can embody their power and gifts as you navigate your life and healing journey.

Take this time for a pause. Rest your mind, body, and spirit. You did a lot today. There's no rush to speed ahead. Let's bookmark this here. Do the thing that's medicine for your soul now. Maybe you can go outside and touch the earth, hug your pet or loved one for co-regulation, do some deep breathing, or listen to your favorite song. I'll see you soon.

PART IV

Simply Existing *Is Often* Dangerous Within a System That Betrays You

I'm wondering about the messages you took into your heart from the systems and institutions you grew up in, and how these messages are now your own self-talk or that of your inner critic. What did you learn about success and how you could "make it"? Oftentimes, the messages Black, Indigenous, and People of Color hear are words fueled with meritocracy: "If you just work hard and do everything you're supposed to do, you'll get everything you want." The belief is that success comes when you work hard. And if it doesn't, it's because you're not trying hard enough. But how many of us know people working their hardest and still coming up short? In fact, many of the hardest working people around the world often come up short, *because the systems they exist in are inequitable.* What if you work really hard and your goals still don't come to fruition? Is it because you "should've worked harder"? Or is it because maybe the structure of the systems you're a part of haven't entirely been built for your success? As I mentioned in an earlier chapter, we all have our own talents and abilities, but not all of us have the same access to resources and opportunities.

And then you hear about the success stories of People of Color, and see White folks using them to negate that racism still exists. They say, "See? There's no more racism because we have Black and Brown people working at our company now." Or "My daughter is married to a Black person, so we can't be racist." I mean, not only are these statements microaggressions, but they're also bandages covering up systemic wounds that remain unaddressed.

As far as success stories are concerned, including your own, I think it's important to ask yourself:

- What did I have to sacrifice to get to where I am?

- What feelings did I have to numb out or suppress?

- What parts of me did I have to hide?

- What parts do I still hide or tone down to fit in?

- What did I have to go through/put up with to finish my education or get my job?

- What do my nervous system and body go through for this success?

I invite you to reflect on what your lived experiences as a Black, Indigenous, and Person of Color have looked like in your places of work (and maybe even difficulty finding work). What has it felt like for you to climb the metaphoric "ladder of success"? And as I say that, how do you define success? What does success look like to you, and how do you know when you've achieved it?

The standards of "success" tend to be blended with capitalism, productivity, and a person's value. You might believe your worth is contingent upon what you can produce, because you've probably heard that from an early age. What messages did you hear when you failed at something? What were the messages told to you about success and your self-worth? Just some things to consider. If you're willing, reflect on the messages you heard about your worthiness growing up in institutions and systems with structures in place that perpetuate oppression. In our final chapters together, we're going to look deeper at the messages you've internalized from the larger culture and system. We're also going to be moving into the fourth and final step of the cultural empowerment approach to healing: living intentionally to change an unjust system. Truth be told, we have a long way to go to dismantle the racist and oppressive systems we all live in, but I believe it's possible even though it won't be easy.

And in the meantime, as you work toward healing your soul from the wounds of these systems, your healing inspires others to do the same. That's right, your essence and motivation for healing are *that* powerful that you will inspire many. Let's spend some time together hearing more stories that may resonate with you. Stories and dynamics that show how systemic oppression impacts your own inner world, and how you can practice living more intentionally to take back your power. Racism, colonialism, and oppression do not have to steal more from you than what has already been stolen. This includes your own sense of Self. Your connection to who you truly are inside, and the collective Self of your community. Many times, we believe that we're flawed and don't measure up because of how we're treated within institutions and the systems surrounding us. Especially when we've experienced discrimination because of how we look, how we love, and who we are. While you may have felt (and feel) othered, been told regularly that you don't belong and that you are broken, let me remind you again of something your Self already knows. You're not broken.

CHAPTER 10

Stories from Within Toxic Environments

We know the systems are dysfunctional, but we are not without hope for having the courage to navigate and ultimately overcome them. A thread throughout this book has been that witnessing our pain helps us have compassion for ourselves and others with similar struggles. Oftentimes a useful way to do that is through inspired-from-life stories about what others have faced and are currently facing. When we put language to the oppression, racism and xenophobia, trauma and abuse being perpetuated against Black, Indigenous, and People of Color in this country and around the world, it can no longer hide in shadow. We see it, we name it, we fight it through radical healing of ourselves and our ancestors, and we continue to reclaim all that we are by living intentionally and embodying courage to dismantle the system. Now we'll explore some scenarios where this toxicity exists, adding context to the adversity that we, and people in our community or who share similar identities to us, are facing. We'll see how complex posttraumatic stress shows up in the lives of others.

One reminder, as I often say throughout this book: always take care of what comes up for you in the ways you need when stories resonate and bring up feelings. Especially because complex posttraumatic stress can separate you from your bodily sensations. You can soothe yourself through practicing deep breathing, lighting a candle or incense, hugging yourself, drinking tea or water, wrapping yourself in a soft blanket, and all the other ways that feel caring to you.

José and Benita's Story (he/him and she/her)

José and Benita were a cisgender couple from El Salvador in their late thirties who migrated with their two children to New York ten years ago. They were forced to abandon their family business in El Salvador because big businesses were taking over the mom-and-pop shops and they were struggling to put food on the table. They arrived in the US only to struggle with racial trauma. They were regularly subjected to racist slurs, looks, and stereotyping at work. They were underpaid and both worked long hours. José worked in a restaurant kitchen as a line cook and Benita was a housekeeper. They were unable to be there for their children as much as they wanted to, and couldn't attend school functions, because to miss work was to lose income or their employment. José and Benita carried cultural legacy burdens of racism and capitalism, and legacy burdens of financial insecurity (to name a few).

Shared Experience: Migrant and Poverty Trauma

When people decide to leave their home country for another, it's often because it's the last resort. The decision to leave family and all you know is far from easy. But a place that's said to promise freedom and opportunity is alluring, especially when you're experiencing food and housing insecurity, poverty, and violence in your homeland. Living in poverty is traumatic. Naturally, fear will have you in survival mode, with your nervous system in fight-or-flight mode, ruminating about hunger or losing your home due to financial insecurity. Usually, the trauma of living in poverty and competing or fighting for food and resources is what forces people to migrate in the first place. Then comes the migration process, and that alone can be scary and traumatic based on the experiences people have when entering a new country. And when they arrive in the US, migrants usually face the hardship of assimilation and acculturation, especially those who are more melanated, have disabilities, are LGBTQIA2S+, and have other intersecting marginalized identities.

Is this part of your story? Or do you know someone who shares José and Benita's experience? Or maybe you were born in the US and also struggle with food and housing insecurity. You may know the hurt of hearing the larger culture tell you that you're "lazy" and need to "work harder" and "not accept government handouts." José and Benita endured so much racial trauma after moving to the US that they began to internalize the messages that they didn't belong. They also felt anxiety, trying to juggle work and supporting their children. It's heartbreaking that families are forced to choose between being present for their children and work, because a loss of income has grave consequences for many.

You might notice you (or your caregiver) share a similar story to José and Benita's, and it might've brought up some feelings. See what you notice in your body and care for yourself in the ways that feel best. When you're ready, let's read about Jules.

Jules's Story (they/them)

Jules was a nonbinary multiracial fifteen-year-old in Brooklyn, New York. Their mom was Black and Asian, and their father was White. At the age of seven, Jules began to see how their White peers and teachers would mistreat them—whether that was being bullied by the other kids or being dismissed by their teachers and faculty. It was at that time that their parents first spoke to them about racism. As Jules got older, they believed they didn't belong because they weren't "Asian enough" or "Black enough" or "White enough." They had always felt othered and didn't fit in anywhere, and this caused a lot of pain. Jules's parents were coming around to accepting Jules's gender fluidity, after first telling them it was a phase they were going through and often misgendering them. Jules was frequently the target of prejudice, and even blatant aggression from strangers in many settings, whether on public transportation or at their retail job. Jules carried cultural legacy burdens of racism, xenophobia, cissexism (discrimination and oppression of transgender, nonbinary, and gender-nonconforming people), and the personal burdens from being bullied and harassed due to the isms they faced.

Shared Experience: Cissexism and Transphobia

Jules's contention with race and belonging isn't unique to them. First, for biracial, multiracial, or mixed-race folks, choosing one racialized identity over the other is difficult and can feel like choosing one important part of you over another. It can often leave you in a weird place of not knowing where you fit in, even if a part of you appreciates being mixed-race. And still, some people struggling with being mixed-race might assimilate to the dominant White culture for survival and a sense of belonging.

Second, we've been conditioned by the larger culture to view the world in a binary, though gender is expansive. In Western culture, we're conditioned with messages about the gender binary from birth and are expected to adopt these expectations: boys are supposed to be tough, girls are encouraged to be soft. The binary social construct was created by colonists and White supremacy culture. ALOK, a gender-nonconforming public speaker, writer, performer, and activist, speaks often about how the gender binary was constructed by colonists to exert power over gender-variant Black and Indigenous peoples after seeing their power.[37] They've also spoken about the cross-dressing laws of the nineteenth century that criminalized gender-nonconforming People of Color for freely expressing gender and living outside the binary, especially transfeminine folks regularly harmed by transmisogyny.

And the anti-trans legislation that's still being instituted harms all transgender and gender-nonconforming people. If you're a gender-nonconforming, Two-Spirit, or transgender person, how has life been for you in the environments you were raised in? How does your nervous system feel around cisgender people?

Jules felt othered in school. Jules endured violence and an attempt at erasure by the cisgender people around them. Challenges for transgender people are more than just finding gender-neutral bathrooms, though that's one important way to be inclusive. There are structural issues within our systems, anti-transgender laws, and institutions that perpetuate violence onto LGBTQIA2S+ communities, and these structural issues are also infused with racism.

Generally speaking, schools can be a source of trauma for Children of Color (and can burden them even more if they hold other marginalized identities). School may not have been a safe place for you. You may have experienced microaggressions and been bullied, labeled, and misunderstood because schools can judge your hardships as pathology rather than seeing your struggle as traumatic stress from oppressive environments.

Gender-nonconforming, Two-Spirit, and transgender people want safety. They want the world to see them in their power, as they are. They also want cisgender folks (myself included) to do their own work with the binary they've internalized that doesn't even let *them* be free. ALOK says anyone can have compassion without fully understanding. I believe that too, because we innately know how to love, and need to continue decolonizing our minds and hearts. Nonbinary and transgender people will need to lead this conversation, and cis folks can open their hearts and listen.

Similar to Jules's story is Camila's journey, who identified as a trans woman having experienced transphobia and colorism in her environment.

Camila's Story (she/her)

Camila was a thirty-year-old Haitian and Dominican transgender woman living in Newark, New Jersey, with her partner. Camila's family was still living in the Dominican Republic. Camila had always heard comments from her parents and grandparents praising her siblings' lighter skin tone, and how beautiful they thought it was. They often told Camila to make sure she dated someone White to *mejorar la raza*, or "improve the race." Camila struggled with low self-esteem since she was a child, and although her partner complimented her often, Camila never believed them. She always believed her siblings were smarter, more attractive, and more competent than her, but could never really identify why. Camila also experienced transphobic comments from several family members, including some who weaponized religion to denounce her gender identity. Camila carried the cultural legacy burden of transphobia and of racism, and legacy burdens of colorism in her family.

Shared Experience: Colorism

Colorism is one of the ways internalized racism is expressed within our own communities. When you've been taught your skin color is unappealing and carries the cultural burdens of racism, you internalize this message and grow to also put that narrative onto others. Colorism was born of racism that we've all taken into our hearts. It has perpetuated anti-Blackness through valuing lighter skin tone over darker skin tone. It is epitomized by the messages you might've heard to "improve the race" by being with someone of the White race (or at least lighter skin), so that any future children could be born lighter, and therefore, seen as valuable and pure—and exist more safely in the world.

Colorism is conveyed through microaggressions; it's passed down in the messages you've received around your curls, locs, or afro not being professional. It's shown in the way you're less favored by your family when you navigate the world in more melanated skin. When you find yourself looking in the mirror wishing you had lighter skin. It's communicated in the words we speak and the language we use when we refer to darkness as diabolical and light as heavenly. And we learn this at a young age. Like Camila, you might see that you're treated differently than siblings or cousins because you're darker, and that doesn't feel good. Nor did it feel good to Camila to endure transphobia within her family (and the outside world), including when they weaponized religion against her. It affected how she saw herself. Camila couldn't see the beauty in herself and was unable to accept compliments from her partner. She internalized racism. How has colorism impacted you and how was it upheld in your family?

Let's speak more about the connection between colorism and internalized racism. This is Khadija's story.

Khadija's Story (she/her)

Khadija was a thirty-three-year-old cisgender woman and mother of two who immigrated from Tunisia with her husband in the mid-2000s and lived in a suburb of Atlanta, Georgia. Khadija was a homemaker while her husband, Youssef, worked as a forklift operator at a distribution center, and they were practicing Muslims. Their son, Sami, was twelve and their daughter, Jasmin, was ten, and both Khadija and Youssef had extremely high expectations for their children academically. While Khadija knew she should make it clear that she loved her children unconditionally, she struggled to move past the pressure to push her kids to stay ahead and to prove themselves in the classroom. Khadija felt this urge to "prove her own and her children's worth" especially strongly because she observed hijab and wore a headscarf, which made her a target for racist rhetoric when she left home. To fight these perceptions in her own mind, Khadija believed she must prove herself as worthy, nonthreatening, and a beneficial member of society who was raising two more beneficial members of society. Khadija carried the cultural legacy burden of racism.

Shared Experience: Internalized Racism

Khadija has faced Islamophobia and has navigated daily microaggressions, including the looks she receives wearing her hijab as people automatically judge her and sometimes see her as a threat. Khadija has felt othered because of her Islamic faith, her Black skin, and her being an immigrant. She puts tons of pressure on herself, and her children, to perform and get good grades out of fear of their falling behind. And I must confess, I also have a part that fears my two Brown children will be mistreated in school and fall behind. And when your children are being educated in institutions that can perpetuate racism, can anyone really blame you?

That visceral feeling and burden you carry of "being behind" is no joke. This feeling of "needing to catch up" or "not fall behind" is common in immigrant families. And oftentimes, it's part of the legacy burdens your family inherited from historical trauma as Black, Indigenous, and People of Color. If your ancestors were enslaved, were colonized, and faced genocide, you may fear being captive, stolen from, denied access, and dismissed or erased, which brings up feelings of urgency to catch up, particularly to White people. Some of this is also fueled by the burden of scarcity we talked about in chapter 8. It's the feeling that you don't have enough time, that there's not enough money, that you haven't studied enough or don't know enough (even after countless hours of studying), and that *your* very essence isn't enough. You might find yourself crying, grieving for your goals that feel unattainable because of internalized racism. You live trying to catch up, chasing an expectation of "enough" that cannot be met because these standards are rooted in White supremacy culture and are insatiable and unrealistic.

Dr. Kenneth and Dr. Mamie Clark, two psychologists who were active in the civil rights movement, did a study referred to as the "doll test" in the 1940s to show the impact of racism on Black children.[38] The study tested how Black children perceived dolls that looked like them, compared to White dolls. It led to proof that children internalize racism. This study has been repeated several times by different people, and in all studies Black children continued to prefer White dolls over Black dolls. Black children chose White dolls over dolls that looked like them because they believed the White dolls were nicer and prettier, and the Black dolls were bad. Let that sink in for a minute.

You internalize racism in the environments you're raised in, from the systems you're a part of, the institutions that teach you, and the laws that govern you. You learn by watching who's more accepted and who's not. You see which skin tones are revered, and which aren't. You see whose actions are criminalized or pathologized, and who gets more compassion. And then, internalized racism begins to manifest in colorism and microaggressions onto others. I'll speak more in the next chapter about the different types of racism and oppression.

Internalized racism can also show up in the form of *imposter syndrome* (feelings of inadequacy, unworthiness, or "fraudulence"). Let's learn about Enrique's story and how imposter syndrome showed up at work and impacted his career and relationship. As you read, I invite you to consider how imposter syndrome has impacted your life.

Enrique's Story (he/him)

Enrique was a fifty-two-year-old Filipino cisgender man living in La Jolla, California. Enrique was a neurosurgeon and was known for his skill and bedside manner, as well as for his innovative research focusing on degenerative diseases of the spine. Enrique grew up in a family that always expected the best from him. His parents put a lot of pressure on him to excel in school, which he did, although they never seemed to be happy, even when he graduated as valedictorian and received a scholarship to Stanford. Enrique's father had wanted to be in the medical field as well, but was discriminated against when he immigrated with Enrique's mother to the US in the late 1960s and wasn't able to afford medical school.

At the time of his residency, Enrique was in the middle of a divorce. He and his wife had both been unfaithful for years, and he dabbled in cocaine and other drugs to try and block out his constant feelings of depression and despair. From an internal family systems lens, his protector parts would come in to help numb his pain. Although Enrique was recognized as a successful neurosurgeon and he genuinely cared for his patients, he always felt like he didn't belong where he was—that he wasn't good enough, that he didn't deserve his accolades, and that there was a ticking clock until the moment he failed and everyone discovered that he was just a fraud. Enrique carried the cultural legacy burden of racism.

Shared Experience: Imposter Syndrome

Have you ever felt like an imposter in your life? The thing about imposter syndrome is that you could have all the degrees in the world, work in a field over a long period of time, be really knowledgeable about something, and you'll *still* feel like you're an imposter and don't belong. Like Enrique, you tell yourself that you're a fraud and if you're found out, you'll lose your job and your support system. You tell yourself that no one will love you. With imposter syndrome, your inner critic becomes loud and is driven by fear, working hard to help you survive the people or things evoking cues of danger in your environment (which can include your own success, people seeing and acknowledging you, or saying nice things to you). Unfortunately, as a survivor of trauma, sometimes you can experience the kindness of others as a threat if it becomes associated with violence and abuse for you.

Imposter syndrome will have you walking into places minimizing your worth and devaluing yourself because of trauma. As a Black, Indigenous, and Person of Color, your imposter syndrome comes from internalized racism because of the cultural legacy burden of racism; it is internalized White supremacy culture. Feeling like you're not enough because of your race. When you and your family have experienced discrimination, it's likely you've internalized the message that you don't belong. And if this is a legacy burden passed down in your family, you might've had critical caregivers who focused solely on your achievements and shamed your struggles.

If that's your story, you probably grew up downplaying your value, your worth, and your knowledge. In adulthood, you may find yourself minimizing compliments and talking yourself out of your power and worthiness. Your inner critic can convey the belief that you're an imposter, and toxic environments can reinforce these feelings. As a Black, Indigenous, and Person of Color, it's common for your inner critic to carry internalized racism and shame you because of it.

I also struggle with imposter syndrome. I used to feel it only in predominantly White spaces. Over time, it grew and I began to feel I didn't belong anywhere. I have parts that tell me I don't deserve praise, and that when people get to know me, they'll realize I don't know enough. These parts have become very loud while writing this book. I've had to give them love because I know they're young and vulnerable parts within me wanting love and acceptance, from the world and my Self. Latine activist, founder of Latina Rebels, and author Prisca Dorcas Mojica Rodríguez talked about her own experience with imposter syndrome in her book *For Brown Girls with Sharp Edges and Tender Hearts*. She shared her challenges surrounding her sense of worth and value because of predominantly White institutions, where the ivory tower was ivory because these spaces weren't designed for the ebony, honey, or café con leche.[39]

It's hard to be a Black, Indigenous, and Person of Color in White institutions that cannot truly validate the excellence and dignity of folks in the global majority when it teaches revisionist histories and creates the school-to-prison pipeline. Children of Color are punished and pushed out of school due to "zero tolerance" policies because of "problem" behaviors that are actually traumatic stress responses.[40] The more Children of Color are punished and pushed out of school, the less they'll learn and the more they'll believe they're bad (and unloved). Institutional racism sets up Children of Color for incarceration when their behaviors are punished and when police are called, rather than being met with curiosity, compassion, secure attachment, and *real* plans for helping them.

Reflection

How's this all landing in your heart? Some of these stories may resonate with you, or you might know people who've lived these experiences. Cultural legacy burdens pollute the air you breathe. And living in toxic environments that perpetuate these cultural burdens actually worsens your personal burdens and symptoms of complex posttraumatic stress, like when you worry about microaggressions or being seen as a threat for just being you. It's hard to live authentically when the world wants you to hide, shrink, or disappear. You might ask, how can I own my fullness? How can I take up space, when every time I try, it's met with backlash or violence?

It isn't lost on me that people of the global majority can be Self-led and fully access their Self-energy, and still have the world oppress them.

Because this world needs a lot of healing, and everyone has to work with their own internalization of racism and oppression.

Let's begin moving into the next chapter and talk more about how we internalize racism and oppression. But before we do, pause for a moment and stretch. Notice what's happening in your body and what emotions, thoughts, or physical sensations might need some attention from you right now. Is your throat or chest tight? Are you fidgety? Just notice and maybe spend some time with what might be coming up for you after reading the stories of people who may share your similar struggles.

Know that the burdens you carry may be heavy, but they're not you. *You are not the burdens you carry.* I hope you can find the courage to slowly and steadily release them. Unburden the parts of you carrying the baggage of supremacy culture. The best revenge you can ever give toxic environments and people who've wounded you is your healing. See you soon.

CHAPTER 11

Disconnecting from the Spirit and Sense of Self

Who are you when you're not carrying your burdens? Because you're not your burdens. Do you know who you were before you took on these burdens? Do you know who you're meant to be? My wish for you is to one day be able to fully connect with your power and all that you are. Because you're not the hurtful things that systems perpetuating racism and oppression have said you are. And you're not your complex posttraumatic stress.

You may have grown up learning helplessness or voicelessness. Because to have a voice can bring rejection or violence upon you. Sometimes you learn this voicelessness in childhood if you aren't allowed to speak up, or if you're hit after speaking up. Sometimes you learn voicelessness in school, where your teachers attempt to dim your creativity, ideas, beliefs, energy, and Self-expression.

One of the hardest times for me in elementary school was the second grade, when my teacher regularly complained to my mother about me and threatened to have me removed from the gifted and talented class because I didn't do her artwork. She complained I was often daydreaming. I wish she had asked why, rather than just judge and punish my behavior and struggle. Had she taken the time to be curious about what was happening within me, why I couldn't pay attention in class, and why I might've wanted to escape reality and dissociate through daydreams, she would've been able to access the sadness carried in my seven-year-old body. Instead, I learned from my second-grade experience that my sadness and choices weren't welcomed. There was no room in school for my feelings and struggles, and there was certainly no grace from my teacher—someone my seven-year-old spirit wanted to please and make proud. Throughout elementary, middle, and high school, I had a mix of White teachers who were amazingly supportive or incredibly harmful. Surely this experience isn't unique to me, but is the reality for many children of the global majority being taught in predominantly White spaces or by teachers who are burned out and teaching in survival mode because of inequities in teacher salaries and treatment.

Then came time to apply for college (I applied last minute because I had no dreams to attend university and was peer-pressured by friends). My dean, a White woman, told me I didn't have what it took to apply to my first-choice college. She told me that my grades weren't good enough to be accepted, and that I should just apply to community college to show that I could handle college courses. I wish I could show her that I was, in fact, accepted to my first-choice university and given a chance. I also wish all Black, Indigenous, and People of Color struggling with complex posttraumatic stress and other mental health issues were given a chance. That the same grace given to the majority of White people could be offered to the global majority trying to navigate racist and oppressive environments for generations.

I'm wondering what you learned about yourself looking through the lens of the world and the systems and institutions you were a part of. What did you learn about difference? I'm also curious about where you've felt a sense of belonging. Was love available to you in the institutions you were in? What did you learn about your race and skin color from caregivers, school, friends, neighbors, and strangers?

As you witness the cultural legacy burden of racism, let's take a deeper look into the layers of racism as they show up for you in your daily life through microaggressions and larger scale macroaggressions. These layers of racism can contribute deeply to dispiritedness and the loss of a sense of Self for you. When you can name these cultural burdens and deeply understand them, compassion can grow and these burdens can slowly begin to lose their power over you as you release them.

Deepening Our Understanding of the Cultural Legacy Burden of Racism

Racism has historically been understood (and defined in the dictionary) as discrimination or prejudice against a person or group based on their racial or ethnic identity. But it's more than that. It's the systemic power that Black, Indigenous, and People of Color aren't given because of their racialized identity.[41] Racism impacts all cultural and legacy burdens that you experience, with the most racial trauma experienced in Black and Indigenous communities. As I've said, racial trauma can create, or exacerbate, complex posttraumatic stress in Communities of Color. Racism is reflected throughout different layers, ideas, and practices that permeate our society in three main ways: systemic, institutional, and interpersonal racism. These three types of racism then lead to a fourth kind, which is your *internalization* of such toxic and false ideas within or about you.

Systemic racism. Systemic racism consists of the racist beliefs, practices, and White supremacist ideals that consciously or unconsciously influence our perceptions; dictate society's institutions; are embedded in the laws that govern us; and impact who receives help and compassion, who is viewed as "good," and who is criminalized and/or deemed unworthy or "bad."

Experiences of "randomized" searches and profiling at ballgames and airports is one example of the way in which White ideals are recognized, preferred, and deemed "safer" than those of the global majority. In a society that's systemically racist, racist ideals compose its global fabric, perpetuating racial inequities against Black, Indigenous, and People of Color within the dominant White culture. It seeps into all other areas of human life, starting with our institutions, creating institutional racism.

Institutional racism. Institutional racism constitutes the discriminatory policies and practices within institutions (e.g., schools, criminal justice systems, organizations) that restrict the global majority from receiving equal access to opportunities and upward mobility in many areas of daily living. It includes underrepresentation of Black, Indigenous, and People of Color in academia; overrepresentation of Black, Indigenous, and Latine people in prisons; poor health care that leads to disproportionately high numbers of the global majority contracting and dying from illnesses like COVID-19; and on and on. Institutional racism is the failure of our society's financial, economic, educational, health care, housing, and community systems to protect and care for Black, Indigenous, and People of Color equitably. Growing up within institutions that perpetuate racism can impact how you see yourself and others, which then has the power to forge interpersonal racism.

Interpersonal racism. Interpersonal racism is defined as the bigotry, personal prejudices, negative perceptions, and/or conscious or unconscious biases communicated in the words and actions of White people against the global majority, and among Communities of Color themselves. Interpersonal racism occurs person to person, including between friends, family and partners, strangers and acquaintances, bosses and colleagues, and neighbors. This layer of racism includes race-based microaggressions—covert or concealed communications to marginalized groups that they're threatening, don't fit in with the dominant culture, and so on—and macroaggressions, which are overt, noticeable discriminatory acts and statements toward a marginalized group. Interpersonal racism in Communities of Color includes things like colorism, which is a direct influence of White supremacy. Interpersonal racism can then lead to your internalizing racism.

Internalized racism. Internalized racism is reflected in the painful beliefs or feelings (i.e., burdens) you hold as a Black, Indigenous, and Person of Color about your appearance; your worth; the way you speak; your ancestral lineages and practices; and other characteristics of your culture. In other words, the hurtful narratives you receive as a Black, Indigenous, and Person of Color from societal systems, institutions, and interpersonal racism blend to form your own narrative about yourself (see figure 3).

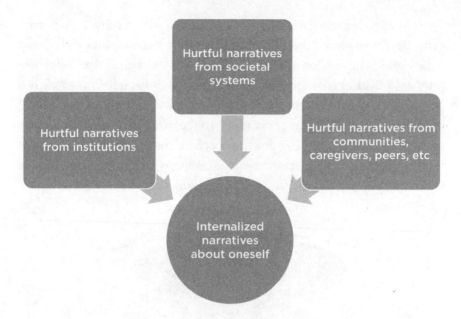

Figure 3: Systemic, institutional, and interpersonal racism lead to internalized racism.

This often leaves you suffering. Internalized racism can look like imposter syndrome, code-switching, or rejecting one's own race in order to survive and be accepted in predominantly White spaces. You can also develop internalized racism, in the form of implicit bias, from what you see in the media. If you're consistently receiving messages that Black and Brown people are bad, you'll naturally create associations that other people who look like you are bad, or that you're bad too—which then becomes internalized racism taught to you by the systems and institutions you're surrounded by.

There's been a plethora of folks discussing the different layers of racism. They've created a variety of ways to illustrate the layers of racism. I'd like to add my own representation here, as this feels closest to how I understand the pervasive nature of racism. The same is also true with systemic oppression.

You can view the three layers of racism as a sort of funnel. Each type of racism "pours into" the next: from the most systemic and widespread beliefs and behaviors of society; to the ways those beliefs and behaviors filter into institutions; and finally to the acts and statements of racism perpetrated on an interpersonal level against Black, Indigenous, and People of Color. All of these forms of racism (with the words and beliefs that come along with them) then filter down to become the internalized feelings of inferiority, shame, pain, resentment, and grief within Communities of Color themselves—like a container catching all that's being poured into it.

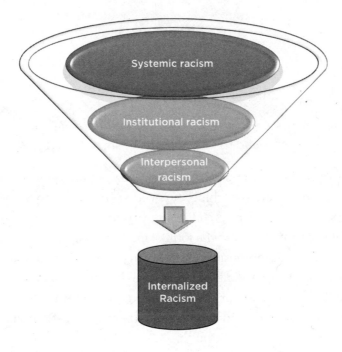

Figure 4: The funnel of racism.

Let's take a moment here. Notice what's up for you. When you're ready, I invite you to do this next practice to reflect on your own internalized racism.

REFLECTION PRACTICE:
Exploring My Internalized Racism

If you feel moved, write down your answers to these questions in your journal. If not, make yourself comfortable wherever you are and just contemplate your responses.

- In what ways have you internalized racism and find it ingrained in the way you see yourself?

- How does internalized racism show up in the language you use?

- How often do you shrink yourself and play small?

You might need to keep coming back to that reflection practice as you continue uncovering the ways internalized racism shows up and how parts of you might then hold yourself back. Especially when it comes to playing small to appease the parts of others intimidated by you or when you're around people trying to overpower you. Talk to those young, tender parts of you that believe you must shrink to be loved, to avoid harm, or to accommodate the fears of others. They need so much of your compassion and tenderness. And they also need your advocacy.

When Connecting with Self-Energy Feels Scary

You lose so much of your inner fire when you spend much of your time trying to extinguish it because the world taught you to fear your fire. On the contrary, your fire is like that of a rocket ship. It helps you launch and propels you forward. Your fire is your passion. It's your courage. It's your love. Your fire is what you share with your ancestors, and it's such a gift if you lean into the messages it has for you. White supremacy culture can have you feeling afraid to embrace your own legacy heirlooms, like your inner fire. But sometimes your fire might say, *Speak up*. Sometimes your fire might say, *This doesn't feel right.* Sometimes your fire helps you take a stand. And that's the thing—racist and oppressive systems will have your fire living in exile so that you *don't* stand.

Complex posttraumatic stress and racist and oppressive systems divorce us from our deepest, most authentic, loving, and compassionate Self. It's important to consider why you might feel scared to embrace your own Self-energy. My friend Rebecca Ching and Dr. Frank Anderson had a conversation on Rebecca's podcast (The Unburdened Leader) on the hardship trauma survivors can experience tuning in to their Self-energy.[42,43] They mentioned that trauma survivors can struggle to feel safe connecting to their own Self-energy, because experiencing the qualities of the Self, like a sense of calm, can feel threatening.

Do you struggle with owning your power and Self-energy because you fear what might happen? It makes sense that you'd be afraid to feel powerful or calm if you were abused or neglected as a child when you exhibited those qualities of Self—such as compassion, creativity, courage, confidence, connectedness, clarity, calmness, and curiosity. As I mentioned in chapter 5, we are all born with a Self. This means, as a child, you have a Self. When you're experiencing abuse or neglect, you learn early on that your Self isn't trustworthy because you were bad. Maybe you were told that *you* caused your abuse. Putting your guard down and connecting to your Self-energy (which embodies those eight qualities) can feel risky to younger parts of you that carry shame and fear of being hurt again.

Sometimes avoiding being calm can be a survival strategy of a protector part of us trying to anticipate the next move in this game of trauma chess. This hypervigilance is a symptom of complex posttraumatic stress. Like those times when you find yourself looking for distractions to help you avoid making hard decisions or being vulnerable. I'm just wanting to normalize any fears you have about being more connected with your Self-energy because racist and oppressive systems haven't allowed you to do that. In fact, your Self and the expression of all your parts have been discouraged, possibly within all three layers of racism. It takes courage to say, "I'm taking my power back and reclaiming who I am." So if I haven't told you enough, I'm glad you're here considering it.

Let's take a moment to pause. Breathe deeply, move your body in the ways that feel comfortable, give yourself an embrace—anything that feels like care to you. As we continue, I'd like to offer you a way to spiritually honor your Self-energy through creating an altar. It can be useful to see an external representation of your Self when you're struggling with internalized racism.

SPIRITUAL PRACTICE:
Make an Altar for Self-Energy

As you continue getting to know who you are at your core, I invite you to externalize your Self, possibly using an altar as a way of reconnecting with and honoring yourself. Set an intention for love and healing.

Step 1: Consider what symbolizes the eight qualities of Self-energy for you. As a reminder, these qualities are compassion, creativity, courage, confidence, connectedness, clarity, calmness, and curiosity. You can also think of places and things that help you feel connected to your core essence and gather any materials that represent them. Feel free to draw and include any pictures that are fitting.

Step 2: Envision who you would be if you weren't carrying cultural burdens of racism and oppression. Gather materials or pictures, draw, or write words that represent yourself unburdened (at your truest form—without the burdens you carry).

Step 3: With your materials, prepare your altar on a shelf, table, or wherever makes sense to you.

Step 4 (optional): Feel free to also represent other parts that you're getting to know better as an ode to your inner world.

May this serve as a reminder that you are not what racist systems say you are. You are not what people who couldn't love you say you are. You are not the painful messages you've internalized.

To Wrap It All Up...

You've been reflecting on how cultural legacy burdens of racism and oppression have deeply impacted your connection to your Self and have also influenced your fear of deeper connection to who you truly are unburdened. Now I want you to begin asking yourself what needs to happen within that'll give you permission to access more of your Self-energy. What would your manager, firefighter, and exiled parts look like if they were free? Sincerely take the time to think about it.

From an internal family systems lens, these three parts fully unburdened are such a powerhouse. Your fully unburdened manager parts would be more confident and in control without feeling overly responsible. They'd be more creative in problem solving and nurturing. Your fully unburdened firefighter parts would be able to self-soothe in healthier ways when the going gets tough and advocate for equity and justice, and they would bring adventure to your life. And your fully unburdened exiled parts—your young parts—would embrace their playfulness, embrace their innocence, and be willing to trust your Self again.[44]

What do you need to get there? I know that racist and oppressive systems don't magically go away. I know that there are plenty of external constraints from these systems. Things happen in life beyond your control that can get in the way of your quality of life. To the best that we can, you and I will need to keep working together to change these unjust systems that have taken from you and from many. But your peace can no longer be an afterthought. Your peace is your *right*, even when they come for it and tell you that you're undeserving. Are you willing to keep trying to find your peace and power? And when you do, are you willing to sit with them, even if you're afraid? I'm confident you will find your way, and that your way will lead to an opening in your vast heart space you may have never known. Or that you're just getting reacquainted with. You *will* embody your power, just as you will embody your peace. As you begin practicing intentionality in thought and behavior, you open the doors to becoming your most authentic Self. In the fourth empowerment step, you'll be writing down your personal promise, or mission statement, to yourself.

If it feels okay, take my words in. Breathe them in when you inhale. I believe you can do this. I believe you *will* do this. I believe in your power to change the world. I believe in your ability to love and your capacity to receive it. I hope my words become part of your mantra as you continue to become your own champion. *You are the meaning of love and wonder, and there is absolutely nothing you need to do to prove your worth.*

Let's move on to our last step of the cultural empowerment approach to healing and help you live more intentionally and connected to your Self-energy. In the meantime, rest your spirit. See you there.

CHAPTER 12

Fourth Empowerment Step: Live Intentionally to Change an Unjust System

You have everything you need within you to heal. You might spend much of your time looking outside of yourself for all the things you can buy, do, take, and receive for you to get better. But the remedy is within. *You* are the source for your healing. You are the medicine for complex posttraumatic stress. And of course, community and love from your environment help restore your sense of belonging and connection to others and your Self.

Can you consider making a promise to yourself? That as you evolve and learn even more about your inner world, you continue recommitting to living authentically and unapologetically? It will require you to get clear on your true nature. It will take you seeing who you really are under all the layers of trauma and burdens. Your clarity on this is so important as you continue exploring what living intentionally and fully looks like for you. What would you rather be doing if you didn't have to heal the wounds of systemic racism and oppression, break generational curses, and disrupt cycles of intergenerational trauma? Think about this for a moment. Whatever images come to mind, see what you need for you to get there. The journey begins by checking in with your inner world, before returning to the outside world and taking actionable steps toward what you yearn for.

Let's begin with connecting more to your true nature. I'd like to start with asking you to try on a few affirmations to see what sticks. Think of three to five things that you like about yourself, whether they embody qualities of your Self-energy (like the eight Cs), or whether they're qualities of parts of you being expressed. For instance, I appreciate my ability to listen and have compassion for others. I also feel grateful that I have the courage (sometimes) to have hard conversations. I appreciate the parts of me that are protective in predominantly White spaces, where I'm doing more emotional labor to exist in that space. They let me know when to pause and when to walk away. Lastly, I feel love for my strong intuition (that admittedly sometimes I don't listen to). What about you? Feel free to just reflect, or write your responses in your journal or on a sheet of paper that you can hang somewhere accessible to you. Let it serve as a reminder that there are qualities of your Self and parts that you appreciate, and can grow more gratitude for.

Now, let's build on the knowledge of who you are. I'd like you to imagine you were writing a biography about yourself. What parts, qualities, or roles feel important to name that help make you who you are? I remember Oprah saying in her life class on the OWN network that we become what we believe. Inspired by a pastor's sermon, she said that the words you say after "I am" follow you.[45] And I think about how we've internalized racism and all the burdens we've absorbed that aren't ours but have adopted from racist and oppressive systems. Especially when burdens can blur the lines of who you believe yourself to be because of trauma. I invite you to reflect and write down what your truest "I am" is.

JOURNALING PRACTICE:
What Is My Truest "I Am"?

As you think about who you are unburdened, write down your responses in your journal or on a sheet of paper. Feel free to type it up if that works for you. You might write, I am thoughtful, I am a dedicated parent, I am hopeful, I am a survivor of trauma, I am healing, I am confident, I am powerful, I am brilliant, I am loving, I am whole, I am responsible, I am playful, I am capable, and more. When that feels complete, read the words aloud to yourself if that's possible for you. Or you can speak them in your mind. If you wrote it on a sheet of paper, consider hanging it somewhere accessible to you. If it's in your journal, bookmark it. Notice what comes up for you as you're acknowledging all that's true about you. Take care of yourself in the ways you need if you notice feeling emotions that want your love and attention. Keep coming back to these words, daily. They can be your mantra, planting seeds of a new Self-talk script that over time bears new fruits that challenge internalized racism and oppression.

The Power of Choice

When there are external constraints, it's really hard to embody Self-energy. When it feels right, even in the smallest of moments, give yourself the permission to embody your love and calm. The world will still be racist, and external constraints may not swiftly change, but you still deserve your care. When external constraints interfere with your ability to feel safe and live authentically as your truest "I am," go inside yourself and find your inner resources. Your bodily sensations, like tension, and your armor protect your most innate qualities as you navigate systemic racism and oppression. Your armor tells you when something doesn't feel right and you need to scan the area (or get to know someone more) for safety. Your armor is valuable and helps keep you safe to the best of its ability, so I wouldn't recommend bulldozing it away. I'm sure there might be parts of you feeling tired of wearing this armor and parts of you that appreciate it for safeguarding your vulnerability.

What matters here is *choice*. Choice, being the unofficial "C" quality of the Self. You can *choose* to find a resource in your self-protection, without overprotecting yourself and shutting out the world. Maybe you want to be guarded in environments where you often experience microaggressions. In this case, call upon the parts of you that can protect your heart and energy. Remember that your protector parts are meaningful and can help your Self.

Sometimes we think we're making a decision that's based on choice, but it's loaded with energy from personal and legacy burdens—for example, when you accept that job offer with a lower wage because you need income, despite knowing that the pay is inequitable. Or when you overcommit yourself at work, in school, or with friends and family because of FOMO (fear of missing out) or feeling overly responsible to "be there." Or when you straighten your natural hair for a special event because you think you look better. Or when you code-switch in predominantly White spaces. These decisions can feel different to your nervous system, and your inner world, if they're coming from conscious choice. Choice helps facilitate a sense of agency. With choice, you release helplessness and make space for power and intention in your life.

Let's do a brief practice on choice. In your journal, write the response that comes to you right now. You can also come back to this anytime you're in need of some reflection.

REFLECTION PRACTICE:
I Choose

In this moment:

- I choose to...

- I am...

- I believe...

- I call upon...

- I feel...

- I'd like...

- I can ask for...

- I have the power to...

In the spirit of intention and choice, I invite you to write your own personal promise. Forward-Facing trauma therapy calls this your mission statement. Dr. Eric Gentry, expert on complex posttraumatic stress and founder of Forward-Facing trauma therapy, asks folks to write a mission statement to help them get clarity on their direction and motivation as they try to be their "best Self" and actualize their dreams, aspirations, and potential.[46]

JOURNALING PRACTICE:
My Mission Statement

You can use your journal or a separate sheet of paper for this practice. When you're ready, begin to write down what you want to claim and seek for yourself. If you want, you can use some of your answers from the previous "I am" practice. Know that your mission statement can evolve over time and you can always add more.

In this mission statement, include:

- what represents the core of who you are

- what is unique to you

- your values and who you promise to continue to be, or what you strive for

- what you want for yourself socially, spiritually, emotionally, and physically

As you write your mission statement, consider all the important roles you play in your life. And most importantly, write this to inspire *you*, not others.

Here's an example:

I am Natalie, a Puerto Rican cis woman who grew up in NYC Baruch Housing and have known much sacrifice. I love singing to music and dancing. I long for more connection to music and dance, and I want to commit to taking more time for myself to do this. I am a survivor of trauma. I am wanting to see myself grow in confidence. I want to speak up more without doubting myself and I want to trust that I know enough. I want to feel loved every day and I want to feel safe to love others. I sometimes hunger for more closeness and want to continue growing my community. I want to continue to develop a deeper connection with my ancestors and their wisdom, and break cycles of intergenerational trauma. I want to be a caring mother and for my kids to know that they are loved by me. I want to feel fully comfortable accepting the compliments of others, and continue loving myself for all that I am. I am complete. I am enough!

When you feel finished, read your mission statement aloud in a mirror, or wherever feels comfortable. You can also choose to speak these words in your mind. Intentionally reading, speaking, or thinking your words is an act of proclaiming your dreams, who you are, and what you wish for in the world. You're reclaiming your right to have a voice that speaks your heart's desires and your truth. This is necessary for Black, Indigenous, and People of Color struggling with complex posttraumatic stress, wanting to connect with their power and sense of Self. You can also choose to "soul gaze" afterward, which is intentionally gazing for several minutes in the mirror, looking into your eyes and experiencing yourself.

Take a deep breath if it feels right here. Stretch. Drink some water and take a pause if you need. When you're ready, let's talk about how you can hold on to your integrity in an unjust system and with people who have hurt you.

REFLECTION PRACTICE:
Holding on to Integrity

Also inspired by Forward-Facing trauma therapy is the reminder to hold on to yourself when you're feeling activated. Remember the power of your choice and agency. Go ahead and bring yourself back to a time when someone was hurtful to you, someone disappointed you, or you experienced a microaggression. If this were to happen again, how would you answer these questions:

- Who do I want to be in this moment?

- How do I want to be in relation to this?

- How do I want to feel with this?

- Who do I want to be when they're not being who I want them to be?

If you react to issues in ways that aren't aligned with your values, or with less access to the qualities of your Self-energy, you're not going to feel too good by the end of it. At some point, you might experience backlash (e.g., anger or disappointment with yourself) and add to the burden of shame you're already carrying. That's why living with intention and making choices from a place of awareness really creates powerful ripple effects of healing and liberation. You get to choose rather than be told. You get to respond rather than react, feeling more in control of yourself. There's opportunity, when you practice *choosing* your responses, to release yourself from the burdens you carry that are impacting the ways you react. When you lay down your burdens, you also begin to let go of your symptoms of complex posttraumatic stress, because they're tied together. Your symptoms are the parts of you communicating the burdens they're carrying.

Embodying the Goals of Internal Family Systems

In time, as you release your burdens, you see more of who you are before you took them on. You gain more access to Self-energy. Unburdening your parts that are holding on to pain and legacy burdens is an essential ritual of IFS. Clearing the energy of your burdens can help you live your life more aligned with who you are and who you're meant to be. After you release your burdens through befriending and witnessing all the parts of you carrying pain and unburdening them through ritual, you'll need to restore trust in your Self-leadership. This way your protector parts can do something else they'd rather be doing, and you can call on them when you *choose* to have them around. After you feel more trusting of your Self, it's important to work on having a relationship with all the parts of you. Your parts will forever be there for your Self, and your Self will always be an ally for your parts. Creating harmony in your inner world can help you gain that inner peace and sense of Self you seek. And last, continuing to show up in the world more Self-led (and ancestor-led) supports your ability to make decisions and act with intention and conscious choice.

To Wrap It All Up...

Living intentionally and pausing to make choices that are most aligned with who you are and who you want to be, especially in difficult moments, helps break cycles of intergenerational trauma, release cultural and legacy burdens, and heal symptoms of complex posttraumatic stress. Because your ancestors were not given choice and power as a result of historical trauma, your efforts to live with intention in unjust systems become cardinal needs. This is your right. This is the food that feeds the soul. And like I said before: when it comes to you, you are the source. Your life of intention is the antidote to the trauma of injustice. Your commitment to live intentionally and authentically in your fullness will inspire others to do the same. The more you unearth your individual and collective power, the more courage you will have to change unjust systems, and rest in the process. You deserve your mental, emotional, physical, and spiritual freedom. Anchor yourself in that truth.

A Vision for the Future:
A Road Map of Resilience
to Help You Stay the Course

I'm so thankful for you, walking alongside this journey with me in the ways you did. Thanks for showing up here in all the ways that felt right for you, honoring yourself and your needs. Thank you for taking this risk to heal and open your heart to my words and maybe even trust them. I appreciate your courage and your presence in this world, and your intention to heal despite all you've been through warms my heart and helps give me hope in the tomorrows ahead. What else do you have to add to this conversation? What more do you want to say about how trauma has impacted you and your community? How do you center your healing and that of your community?

Now more than ever is the time for our collective healing—a healing so desperately needed as a pandemic and dual racial and climate reckonings have highlighted just how deep the fissures of inequity, racism, oppression, exploitation, and White supremacy culture go in this country and the world. We will not let it go on any longer. We will fight for ourselves, our loved ones, our ancestors, and our collective futures. We *will* dismantle and mend.

Many are fighting, leading the charge for different issues that circle back to a unifying demand—equity, justice, liberation, and dignity. Indigenous land and water protectors are putting their bodies on the line and getting arrested to stop the Line 3 oil pipeline or pepper sprayed to keep trees from getting cut down in Canada. Black Lives Matter, Until

Freedom, and Movement for Black Lives have been on the front lines for years speaking out against police brutality, systemic racism, and racial injustice. There are movements fighting the anti-transgender legislation being introduced in several states across the US. There's also activism around climate change. I'm in awe, that as we carry the burdens of historical trauma and the cultural legacy burdens of our world, we remain courageous and take a stand. Taking a stand feels like the epitome of love. Love takes a stand, letting courage lead the way.

In my vision for the future, I see everyone making strides toward their healing. The disease of White supremacy no longer exists and we're all healing from its toxins. I see us all being open and honest about our own parts that hold implicit bias, rather than trying to rationalize or exile them. In this envisioned future, your spirit is fed every day by community, and you smile and belly laugh unapologetically. You are being your most authentic Self, and your tears are being met with tenderness. You tell me you finally feel safe. You walk right into a room and *know* that you belong and can take up space there. My vision for the future is still unfolding, and it helps me hold on to hope for our unshakable courage and becoming.

Your resilience thrives when you allow yourself to dream and imagine. When you engage with your creativity, you're less in a threat response. Creativity, and all the qualities of your Self, are essential for Self-leadership and intentional living, so that you have *choice*. Having choice is empowering, and feeling powerful helps you trust your Self again. This is what is needed to confront racist and oppressive systems and work through your struggle with complex posttraumatic stress.

I invite you to do one last practice with me, your resilience road map, to help you stay the course. If you've ever created a vision board (a board with illustrations or words that detail your dreams and aspirations), I'm curious about what you chose to include there and why it's important. Does it inspire you to go even deeper about the future your heart is longing for?

JOURNALING PRACTICE:
Building Your Resilience Road Map

Step 1: In your journal or on a sheet of paper, write down what you envision for the future. As you visualize it, what do you want for the collective? Consider your values in your vision (maybe closeness, forgiveness, honesty, love, justice, or unity). After you've mulled it over and written your answer, take a moment to consider what you would also like to see for your Self.

Step 2: As you think about how to journey the world with this vision in your heart, consider how you will use the four empowerment steps to help you. I've written some key questions from each empowerment step for your reflection. You can use this as a quick guide to the empowerment steps and return to it when you're having an off day and need prompts to help facilitate reflection and move you from your threat response to curiosity and calm. Doing this can help you create space within you for more perspective on dealing with an issue, and maybe even more openheartedness toward your parts and the parts of others.

- **First Empowerment Step: Use Your Body to Regulate Your Own Well-Being**

  How will you listen to your body? In what ways will you care for your bodily sensations when you're hurting to slow down your threat response? It's important for you to get into the habit of only going into a threat response when you truly need it. How will you bring a sense of safety back into your body today?

- **Second Empowerment Step: Mend Shame and Shaming Beliefs with Self-Compassion**

  Now consider how you will tend to shame and your inner critic. Who in your past are you emulating when you're saying mean things to yourself? How will you seek to understand and offer your protector parts and most vulnerable parts compassion? How will you convey the same patience and gentleness to yourself that you give to others? Tend to the younger parts of you needing your attention.

- **Third Empowerment Step: Access the Energy of Your Ancestors' Wisdom**

  How can you be both Self-led and ancestor-led? What can you do to stay connected with your ancestors, known and unknown? How will you continue practicing ancestral reverence? What legacy resources can you hold on to or call upon when you're having a tough time? Engage in ceremonial releasing rituals if you need to unburden what you're carrying.

- **Fourth Empowerment Step: Live Intentionally to Change an Unjust System**

  Who do you want to be when the world isn't being what you want it to be? And, who do you want to be when the people you love aren't always who you want them to be? Start there. See yourself practicing *choosing* how you respond, rather than reacting how you do when you're overwhelmed. Get clear about how you want your Self-leadership to look every day.

Equipped with your resilience road map, you now have a plan in place next time you're presented with a potentially activating experience. And the most soulful part is that when *we* are regulated, and when *we* are courageous in embodying our fullness, we transmit that healing, love, compassion, and regulation to all those we come in contact with. When you move through the world Self-led, your heart is open and you can connect more with others. You're literally helping to heal your communities and the planet around you not only through your actions and activism to fight these unjust systems, but also through your *very existence in that environment in a regulated and resilient body and mind.*

I also want to say that if you haven't done any of the practices yet, that's okay. You can when you're ready, or perhaps for you it works best to let these ideas percolate rather than write them down. I trust that your way is the way for you. Not everyone heals at the same pace and not everything works for everyone. And sometimes things need to come at the right season of your life. As a student of life, I understand that learning happens in layers, so we often need to go back and read things again, and see what we missed, can gain, or can recharge with.

If there's anything you get from me, please let it be that I sincerely believe in you and your ability to heal. I believe in your heart and your power even as racism and supremacy culture attempt to other you. We need each other in this fight for freedom and that your healing is yours and can't be taken from you. No one has dibs on your healing, except you. I want to offer you the words my ancestors once told my exiled seven-year-old inner child in a therapy session: "Embrace what they taught you to hate about yourself."

If left to the devices of supremacy culture and oppressive systems, you'd live the rest of your life with a long list of reasons why you're not good enough. Rip that shit up. Set it on fire in your mind if you need to. Release it to the elements. You will no longer settle for scraps and disillusionment of who you're not. You know who you are deep within. Nothing you do will ever be good enough for a system that's designed to scapegoat and shrink you. So hold on to yourself. Hold on to who you are and what makes you different. Hold on to your culture and your people. Hold on to your ancestral connection and your legacy resources. Hold on to your right to heal. I need you to know that healing is possible. It may not always feel like it, but as you continue to release the burdens you carry, you can connect more with your Self and your community. Your connection with community strengthens the collective Self of your community. With more clarity, courage, compassion, curiosity, connectedness, and love, we can lead with intention and choice. We can rise and rebuild.

We create new legacies and heal in community when we love each other through our action and we stand together for our liberation. Our soul liberation supports our collective liberation, and our collective liberation frees our soul. There's power in numbers and unity and love. And there are people rooting for you, including your ancestors within and around you. There are people unwavering in the fight for peace, justice, and equity. We can reimagine and move toward decolonizing every fiber of our mind, spirit, beliefs, and systems that created and perpetuated racialized trauma and cultural legacy burdens. We got this together. We can hold this together. I will continue to stand with you through it all. As so many others will too. You're not alone. You have community here. I believe in you. And I love you and all of your parts that got you here and help you travel along the way. Release your burdens and travel light.

Acknowledgments

I couldn't have written this book at the start of a pandemic, meeting with clients, and juggling motherhood if it weren't for the support of my community. There are so many people who have contributed to my writing journey—offering their affirming words, reminding me of my gifts, seeing and loving me.

First and foremost, I really need to thank my children—for lending their mother to birth this manuscript. I didn't realize all it would take, and my children graciously accepted the challenge. To my husband, thank you for stepping up and being there in all the moments I needed you to be. And to my mother and stepdad, I'm eternally grateful to you for being on this wild ride. Although this period was filled with many ups and downs, you all have been my rock. To my ancestors, thanks for having my back.

I also want to express gratitude to my mentor, Dr. Eric Gentry, for cheering me along the way and for your wisdom. And, I'm feeling deep appreciation for all my mentors and peers within the internal family systems community who continue to encourage my growth and lift me up.

To my clients: I'm forever changed by your stories. Thank you for trusting me with your heart.

Finally, I'm appreciating *all* my friends. Thank you for being there for me in all the ways you were. I love you all.

Resources

Please refer to the list below for resources that can aid you in receiving proper care and establishing safe surroundings.

Directories (and some Mental Health Organizations) with Trauma-Informed Practitioners:

Asian Mental Health Collective: https://www.asianmhc.org/therapists-us

Ayana Therapy: https://www.ayanatherapy.com

Black Therapists Rock: https://www.blacktherapistsrock.com

Clinicians of Color: https://www.cliniciansofcolor.org

Inclusive Therapists: https://www.inclusivetherapists.com

Latinx Therapy: https://latinxtherapy.com

Melanin and Mental Health: https://www.melaninandmentalhealth.com

Open Path Collective: https://www.openpathcollective.org

The Society of Indian Psychologists: https://www.nativepsychs.org

Therapy for Black Girls: https://www.therapyforblackgirls.com

Therapy for Latinx: https://www therapyforlatinx.com

Therapy in Color: https://www.therapyincolor.org

Homelessness Resources:

National Coalition for the Homeless: https://www.nationalhomeless. org

National Runaway Safeline: 800-786-2929; https://www.1800runaway. org

Intimate Partner Violence Resources:

Deaf Abused Women's Network (DAWN): https://www.deafdawn.org

National Center on Violence Against Women in the Black Community: 844-778-5462; https://www.ujimacommunity.org

National Domestic Violence Hotline: 800-799-7233; 800-787-3224 (TTY); https://www.thehotline.org

Safe Horizon Domestic Violence Hotline: 800-621-4673; https://www.safehorizon.org

LBGTQIA2S+ Needs Resources:

FORGE (resources for trans+ survivors of violence and their loved ones): https://www.forge-forward.org

GLBT National Help Center: 888-843-4564

National Queer and Trans Therapists of Color Network (NQTTCN): https://www.nqttcn.com

Sayftee: https://www.sayftee.com

Society for Sexual, Affectional, Intersex, and Gender Expansive Identities (SAIGE): https://www.saigecounseling.org

The Trevor Project Lifeline (24/7/365 connection to LGBTQIA2S+-related crisis support): 866-488-7386; https://www.thetrevorproject. org

Trans Lifeline: 877-565-8860

Sexual Abuse/Incest Resources:

MaleSurvivor: https://www.malesurvivor.org

Rape, Abuse, and Incest National Network (RAINN): https://www. rainn.org; Spanish: https://www.rainn.org/es

Survivors of Incest Anonymous: https://www.siawso.org

Suicide and Self-Harm Resources:

Crisis Text Line: Text SHARE to 741741 (24/7/365 connection to a crisis counselor); https://www.crisistextline.org

Disaster Distress Helpline (24/7/365 crisis counseling for emotional distress): 800-985-5990; text TALKWITHUS to 66746

National Suicide Prevention Lifeline: 800-273-8255; 800-799-4889 (TTY); Spanish: 888-628-9454; https://www.suicidepreventionlife line.org

Endnotes

1   Perry, B. D., and O. Winfrey. 2021. *What Happened to You? Conversations on Trauma, Resilience, and Healing.* New York: Flatiron Books.

2   Schwartz, R. C., and M. Sweezy. 2020. *Internal Family Systems Therapy.* 2nd ed. New York: The Guilford Press.

3   Gentry, J. E. 2016. *Forward-Facing® Trauma Therapy: Healing the Moral Wound.* Sarasota, FL: Compassion Unlimited.

4   Gentry, J. E. 2021. *Treating Complex PTSD.* [MOOC]. Udemy. https://www.udemy.com/course/treating-complex-ptsd.

5   Dana, D. 2018. *The Polyvagal Theory in Therapy: Engaging the Rhythm of Regulation.* New York: W.W. Norton & Company.

6   Menakem, R. 2017. *My Grandmother's Hands: Racialized Trauma and the Pathway to Mending Our Hearts and Bodies.* Las Vegas, NV: Central Recovery Press.

7   Perry, B. D., and O. Winfrey. 2021. *What Happened to You? Conversations on Trauma, Resilience, and Healing.*

8   Siegel, D. J., and T. P. Bryson. 2012. *The Whole Brain Child: 12 Revolutionary Strategies to Nurture Your Child's Developing Mind.* Brunswick, Victoria: Scribe Publications.

9   Anderson, F. 2021. *Transcending Trauma: Healing Complex PTSD with Internal Family Systems.* Eau Claire, WI: Pesi Publishing.

10   Pace, K. 2016. "Understanding the 'Upstairs' and 'Downstairs' Brain." Michigan State University Extension. Retrieved November 2021 from https://www.canr.msu.edu/news/understanding_the_upstairs_and _downstairs_brain

11   Gentry, J. E. 2021. *Treating Complex PTSD*. [MOOC].

12   Ann Sinko, Online IFS Intensive Training on Shame, Anxiety, and Depression, January 22, 2022.

13   Dana, D. 2018. *The Polyvagal Theory in Therapy: Engaging the Rhythm of Regulation*. New York: W. W. Norton & Company.

14   Benazzo, Z., and M. Benazzo (Directors). 2021. *The Wisdom of Trauma* [Film]. Science and Nonduality.

15   Comas-Díaz, L., G. N. Hall, and H. A. Neville. 2019. "Racial Trauma: Theory, Research, and Healing: Introduction to the Special Issue." *American Psychologist* 74, no. 1: 1–5. http://dx.doi.org/10.1037 /amp0000442.

16   Anderson, F. 2021. *Transcending Trauma: Healing Complex PTSD with Internal Family Systems*.

17   Gentry, J. E. 2016. *Forward-Facing® Trauma Therapy: Healing the Moral Wound*.

18   Pastor, M. 2021. *Trailheads to Transformation: IFS Institute Continuity Circle*. [MOOC]. IFS Institute. https://ifs-institute.com /online-learning.

19   Frank Anderson, Online IFS Intensive Training on IFS, Trauma, and Neuroscience, June 5, 2021.

20   Pastor, M., and J. Gauvain. 2020. *Internal Family Systems Institute Level 1 Training Manual*. Oak Park, IL: Trailhead Publications.

21   Gentry, J. E. 2016. *Forward-Facing® Trauma Therapy: Healing the Moral Wound*.

22   Brown, B. (Host). 2020, June 30. "Brené on Shame and Accountability." [Audio podcast episode]. In *Unlocking Us*. Parcast Network. https://brenebrown.com/podcast/brene-on-shame-and -accountability.

23   Schwartz, R. C. 2021. *No Bad Parts: Healing Trauma and Restoring Wholeness with the Internal Family Systems Model*. Boulder, CO: Sounds True.

24   Perry, B. D., and O. Winfrey, O. *What Happened to You? Conversations on Trauma, Resilience, and Healing.*

25   Pastor, M., and J. Gauvain. 2020. *Internal Family Systems Institute Level 1 Training Manual.*

26   Menakem, R. (n.d.). "Social Trauma and Embodied Freedom." Rooted Global Village. Retrieved December 2021 from https://www .rootedandembodied.com/resmaa-menakem-racialized-trauma.

27   Anderson, F. 2021. *Transcending Trauma: Healing Complex PTSD with Internal Family Systems* [video].

28   Gentry, J. E. 2016. *Forward-Facing® Trauma Therapy: Healing the Moral Wound.*

29   Benazzo, Z., and M. Benazzo (Directors). 2021. *The Wisdom of Trauma* [Film].

30   Nguyen, T., D. H. Abney, D. Salamander, B. I. Bertenthal, and S. Hoehl. 2021. "Proximity and Touch Are Associated with Neural but not Physiological Synchrony in Naturalistic Mother-Infant Interactions." *Neuroimage* 244, no. 118599: 1–8. https://doi.org/10.1016/j.neuroimage .2021.118599.

31   Perry, B. D., and E. P. Hambrick. 2008. "The Neurosequential Model of Therapeutics." *Reclaiming Children and Youth* 17, no. 38: 38–43. https://citeseerx.ist.psu.edu/viewdoc/download?doi=10.1.1.631.3271&rep =rep1&type=pdf.

32   Anderson, F. 2021. *Transcending Trauma: Healing Complex PTSD with Internal Family Systems.*

33   Perry, B. D., and O. Winfrey. 2021. *What Happened to You? Conversations on Trauma, Resilience, and Healing.*

34   Foor, D. 2017. *Ancestral Medicine: Rituals for Personal and Family Healing.* Rochester, VT: Bear & Company.

35   Chris Burris, Online IFS Level 3 Training Program, October 7, 2021.

36   Medina, L., and M. R. Gonzalez, eds.. 2019. *Voices from the Ancestors: Xicanx and Latinx Spiritual Expressions and Healing Practices.* Tucson, AZ: The University of Arizona Press.

37   Vaid-Menon, A. 2020. *Beyond the Gender Binary.* New York: Penguin Workshop.

38   NAACP Legal Defense and Educational Fund, Inc. (n.d.). "A Revealing Experiment: Brown v. Board and 'The Doll Test.'" NAACP. Retrieved September 2020 from https://www.naacpldf.org /ldf-celebrates-60th-anniversary-brown-v-board-education/significance -doll-test.

39   Rodriguez-Mojica, P. D. 2021. *Brown Girls with Sharp Edges and Tender Hearts.* New York: Seal Press.

40   American Civil Liberties Union. (n.d.). "School-to-Prison Pipeline." American Civil Liberties Union. Retrieved November 2021 from https:// www.aclu.org/issues/juvenile-justice/school-prison-pipeline.

41   DeGruy, J. 2017. *Post Traumatic Slave Syndrome: America's Legacy of Enduring Injury and Healing.* Portland, OR: Joy DeGruy Publications Inc.

42   Frank Anderson, Challenging the Fear of Rejection and Leading with Vulnerability- Part 1, interview by Rebecca Ching, The Unburdened Leader Podcast, May 21, 2021, audio, https://podcasts.apple.com/us /podcast/the-unburdened-leader/id1508203253?i=1000522643095

43   Rebecca Ching, Text message to author, June 2021.

44   Pastor, M., and J. Gauvain. *Internal Family Systems Institute Level 1 Training Manual.*

45   OWN. 2012, August 28. *Why Oprah Says the Words "I Am" Matter: Oprah's Lifeclass.* [Video]. https://www.youtube.com/watch?v=6iwn Lmh-iPA.

46   Gentry, J. E. 2016. *Forward-Facing® Trauma Therapy: Healing the Moral Wound.*

Natalie Y. Gutiérrez, LMFT, is founder of Mindful Journeys Marriage & Family Therapy PLLC, and a licensed marriage and family therapist working primarily with BIPOC (Black, Indigenous, People of Color) survivors of complex trauma—ranging from racial trauma, sexual trauma, attachment trauma, and intergenerational trauma. Natalie is a certified internal family systems therapist and prospective trainer at the IFS Institute. Natalie's individual and group healing work blends the intersections of psychotherapy, activism, and curanderismo. She has more than 23,000 followers on Instagram, where she shares her journey of healing and empowerment. She currently resides in New York, NY.

Foreword writer **Jennifer Mullan, PsyD,** is a clinical psychologist and published author. She currently serves communities as a consultant, therapeutic coach, and ancestral wound worker who seeks to unpack the oppressive legacy of modern mental health practices, particularly for Queer, Indigenous, Black and Brown People of Color (QIBPOC). She has been featured in *Allure, GQ, Cosmopolitan,* on *The Today Show,* and more.

MORE BOOKS from
NEW HARBINGER PUBLICATIONS

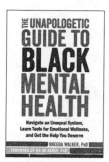

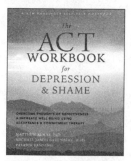

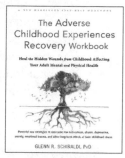

Did you know there are **free tools** you can download for this book?

Free tools are things like **worksheets, guided meditation exercises**, and **more** that will help you get the most out of your book.

You can download free tools for this book—whether you bought or borrowed it, in any format, from any source—from the New Harbinger website. All you need is a NewHarbinger.com account. Just use the URL provided in this book to view the free tools that are available for it. Then, click on the "download" button for the free tool you want, and follow the prompts that appear to log in to your NewHarbinger.com account and download the material.

You can also save the free tools for this book to your **Free Tools Library** so you can access them again anytime, just by logging in to your account! Just look for this button on the book's free tools page.

+ Save this to my free tools library

If you need help accessing or downloading free tools, visit **newharbinger.com/faq** or contact us at **customerservice@newharbinger.com**.